NINJA FOODI GRILL COOKBOOK

Lory Smill

Ninja Foodi Grill Cookbook

TABLE OF CONTENTS

CHAPTER 6: BEEF, PORK, AND LAMB 62

CHAPTER 7: VEGETABLE AND SIDES............78

CHAPTER 8: FISH AND SEAFOOD..................94

Introduction

The Ninja Foodi Grill is the cooking tool that all the hip cookers and chefs have been waiting for. In an age when "clean eating" has become a buzzword, this device demands attention. Ninja Foodi grill is a versatile cooking tool that gives you the freedom to make your own meals, customized to your tastes and dietary needs, without spending hours in long lines or ordering from out-of-town restaurants.

Ninja Foodi Grill will revolutionize the way we cook at home and how we eat out. The whole system is designed to help you take control of your food preparation process. The ninja Foodi grill has special features that will help you play around with the composition of your meals, whether it is making food for the entire family in the right portions or preparing a single meal for yourself. Ninja Foodi Grill allows you to cook in your own kitchen in an easy way that saves time and energy, without sacrificing any flavor.

Ninja Foodi Grill's patented design allows for up to 600°F temperature capability. By using a combination of infrared heating and convection airflow means you can enjoy perfectly-browned grill marks on foods from chicken to fish to beef, without the same risk of flare-ups that you get from a traditional indoor grill. The infrared heat distributes itself evenly across the surface of your food, allowing for an even cooking process.

Ninja Foodi Grill can be used indoors or outdoors. With its sleek body, it doesn't need a lot of space to fit on your kitchen counter. It is a full-sized indoor grill that will make a unique addition to any home and kitchen, regardless of whether you live in an apartment or a mansion.

The Ninja Foodi Grill can be used by everyone in the family and is very easy and safe to use and clean. No more dirty pots and pans, no more burning grill marks, no more running to the stove every few minutes while your food cooks. It can be used by everyone in the family and is very easy and safe to use and clean. No more dirty pots and pans, no more burning grill marks, no more running to the stove every few minutes while your food cooks. You can start cooking at 6 pm and have your food ready for dinner at 6:15 pm. The Ninja Foodi Grill cuts down on your time in the kitchen by up to 50%!

Ninja Foodi Grill provides an amazing choice of cooking options, giving you the freedom to cook your food however you want it. You get six unique cooking methods including Toss and Stir, Flat Top, Crisp and Sear, Indoor BBQ, Panini Press, and NINJA-Q. These features allow you to take your meals to another level without having to leave home. You can prepare healthy foods tailored to your tastes while enjoying the versatility of indoor grilling.

The Ninja Foodi Grill can grill anything! You can cook healthy food in minutes with the highest quality indoor grill in the world. Leave your old, boring cooking tools at home when you get a Ninja Foodi Grill! The options are limitless.

The Ninja Foodi Grill has several accessories that are specially designed to complement your cooking needs. Once you have your own ninja Foodi, there is no need for any other tool around the kitchen. The accessories will help you to prepare delicious meals for yourself and your family.

Ninja Foodi Grill's accessories may come in different colors. You can choose one based on your preference or buy the set with different colors to add more fun to your cooking experience.

CHAPTER 1:

How To Use The Machine For Beginners?

When you cook for the first time with your Ninja Foodi Grill, you must first wash the detachable cooking parts with warm soapy water to remove any oil and debris. Let them air dry and place them back inside once you are ready to cook. An easy-to-follow instruction guide comes with each unit, so make sure to go over it before cooking.

Locate your grill on a level and secure surface. Leave at least 6 inches of space around it, especially at the back where the air intake vent and air socket are located. Ensure that a splatter guard is installed whenever the grill is in use. This is a wire mesh that covers the heating element on the inside of the lid.

For grilling:

- Plug your unit into an outlet and power on the grill.
- Use the grill grate over the cooking pot and choose the grill function. This has four default temperature settings of low at 400°F, medium at 450°F, high at 500°F and max at 510°F.
- Set the time needed to cook. You may check the grilling cheat sheet that comes with your unit to guide you with the time and temperature settings. It is best to check the food regularly depending on the doneness you prefer and to avoid overcooking.
- Once the required settings are selected, press start and wait for the digital display to show "add food." The unit will start to preheat similar to an oven and will show the progress through the display. This step takes about 8 minutes.
- If you need to check the food or flip it, the timer will pause and resume once the lid is closed.
- The screen will show "Done" once the timer and cooking have been completed. Power off the unit and unplug the device. Leave the hood open to let the unit cool faster.

For roasting:

- Remove the grill grates and use the cooking pot that comes with the unit. You may also purchase their roasting rack for this purpose.
- Press the roast option and set the timer between 1 to 4 hours depending on the recipe requirements. The Foodi will preheat for 3 minutes regardless of the time you have set.
- Once ready, place the meat directly on the roasting pot or rack.
- Check occasionally for doneness. A meat thermometer is another useful tool to get your meats perfectly cooked.

For baking:

- Remove the grates and use the cooking pot.
- Choose the bake setting and set your preferred temperature and time. Preheating will take about 3 minutes.
- Once done with preheating, you may put the ingredients directly on the cooking pot or you may use your regular baking tray. An 8-inch baking tray can fit inside as well as similar-sized oven-safe containers.

For Air Frying/Air Crisping:

- Put the crisper basket in and close the lid.
- Press the "Air Fry" option, then the "Start" button. The default temperature is set at 390°F and will preheat at about 3 minutes. You can adjust the temperature and time by pressing the buttons beside these options.
- If you do not need to preheat, just press the "Air Fryer" button a second time and the display will show you the "Add Food" message.

- Put the food inside and shake or turn it every 10 minutes. Use oven mitts or tongs with silicone tips when doing this.

For dehydrating:

- Place the first layer of food directly on the cooking pot.
- Add the crisper basket and add one more layer.
- Choose the dehydrate setting and set the timer between 7 to 10 hours.
- You may check the progress from time to time.

For cooking frozen foods:

- Choose the medium heat, which is 450°F using the grill option. You may also use the Air Fryer option if you are cooking fries, vegetables, and other frozen foods.
- Set the time needed for your recipe. Add a few minutes to compensate for the thawing.
- Flip or shake after a few minutes to cook the food evenly.

Oil	Smoke Point ºF	Smoke Point °C
Refined Avocado Oil	520ºF	270°C
Safflower Oil	510ºF	265ºC
Rice Bran Oil	490ºF	254ºC
Refined or Light Olive Oil	465ºF	240ºC
Soybean Oil	450ºF	232ºC
Peanut Oil	450ºF	232ºC
Ghee or Clarified Butter	450ºF	232ºC
Corn Oil	450ºF	232ºC
Refined Coconut Oil	450ºF	232ºC
Safflower Oil	440ºF	227ºC
Refined Sesame Oil	410ºF	210ºC
Vegetable Oil	400-450ºF	204-232ºC
Beef Tallow	400ºF	204ºC
Canola Oil	400ºF	204ºC
Grapeseed Oil	390ºF	199ºC
Unrefined or Virgin Avocado Oil	375ºF	190ºC
Pork Fat or Lard	370ºF	188ºC
Chicken Fat or Schmaltz	375ºF	190ºC
Duck Fat	375ºF	190ºC
Vegetable Shortening	360ºF	182ºC
Unrefined Sesame Oil	350ºF	177ºC
Extra Virgin or Unrefined Coconut Oil	350ºF	177ºC
Extra Virgin Olive Oil	325-375ºF	163-190ºC
Butter	302ºF	150ºC

CHAPTER 2:

Tips On Machine Maintenance

Components are dishwasher-safe and are fabricated with a non-stick ceramic coating, to make clean-up and maintenance easier. Plus, the grill conveniently comes with a plastic cleaning brush with a scraper at the other end.

Cleaning Tips

1. Let the grill cool down completely and ensure that it is unplugged from the power outlet before trying to clean the unit.
2. Take out the splatter guard, grill grates, and cooking pot, and soak in soapy water for a few hours to let the debris soften and make cleaning easier. Wash only the removable parts.
3. Gently brush off dirt and debris using the plastic brush that comes with your grill. Use the other end of the brush to dislodge food in hard-to-reach areas.
4. Let the parts dry thoroughly.
5. Clean the insides and exterior of the unit with a clean damp cloth.

Maintenance Tips

1. Always keep your unit clean, especially before putting in a new batch for cooking. You should clean the parts and the unit after each use.
2. Never use cleaning instruments or chemicals that are too harsh and can damage the coating.
3. Keep the electrical cords away from children and any traffic in your kitchen.
4. Avoid getting the unit and electrical components wet and place them away from areas that constantly get soaked or damp.
5. Always unplug the unit when not in use.

Troubleshooting

1. **Smoke coming out of the grill.** Although the Ninja Foodi is virtually smokeless as advertised, you may see some smoke from time to time for several reasons.
    a. One is the type of oil you use for cooking. Ideally, canola, grape seed, and avocado oil should be used since they have a high smoke point. This means that they do not produce smoke or burn at high temperatures. Other oils with high smoke points include corn, almond, safflower, sesame, and sunflower oils.
    b. Another reason is the accumulation of grease at the bottom of the pot. If you continuously cook foods that produce a lot of grease and oil, this will burn and create smoke. Empty and clean the pot before cooking the next batch.
2. **The grill is showing "Add Food."** This means that the unit has finished preheating and that you can now put food inside the grill.
3. **The control panel is showing "Shut Lid."** Try opening the lid and closing it securely until the message is gone.
4. **Unit is unresponsive and only showing "E" on the panel.** Your unit is damaged and you need to contact customer service.

CHAPTER 3:

Breakfast

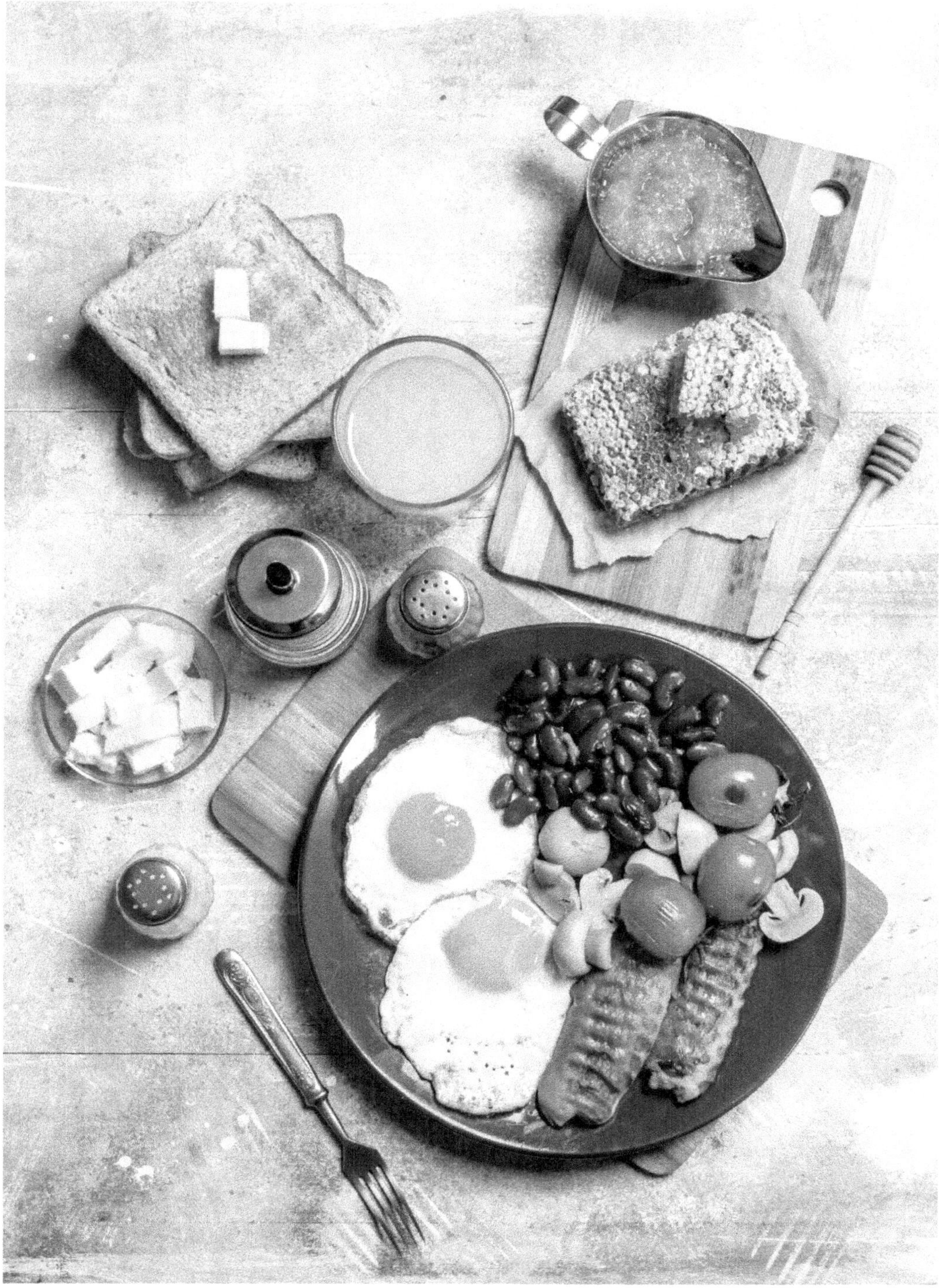

1. Bistro Breakfast Sandwiches

Preparation time: 10 minutes
Cooking time: 12 minutes
Serving: 2
Ingredients:

- 2 tsp. butter
- 4 large eggs, beaten
- 4 hearty Italian bread slices
- 1/8 tsp. salt
- 1/8 tsp. black pepper
- 4 oz. smoked Gouda, cut in 4 slices
- 1 medium pear, sliced
- 4 strips of Canadian bacon, cooked and sliced
- 1/2 cup fresh baby spinach

Directions:

1. Sauté eggs with 1 tsp. butter in a skillet on medium heat.
2. Spread the eggs on top of 2 bread slices.
3. Add black pepper, salt, cheese slices, pear slices, spinach, and bacon on top of the egg.
4. Then place the other bread slices on top.
5. Select the "Grill" Mode, set the temperature to MAX.
6. Use the arrow keys on the display to select the time to 8 minutes.
7. Press the START/STOP button to initiate preheating.
8. Once preheated, place the sandwiches in the Ninja Foodi Grill.
9. Flip the sandwiches once cooked halfway through.
10. Slice and serve warm.

Nutrition:

- Calories: 629
- Fat: 33 g
- Sodium: 1510 mg
- Carbs: 44 g
- Fiber: 3.9 g
- Sugar: 3 g
- Protein: 38 g

2. Delicious Banana Bread

Preparation time: 10 minutes
Cooking time: 40 minutes
Serving: 12
Ingredients:

- 4 ripe bananas, mashed
- 1/4 cup butter, melted
- 1 tsp. baking soda
- 1 tsp. baking powder
- 1 1/4 cups flour
- 1 tsp. vanilla
- 1 cup sugar
- 1/2 tsp. salt

Directions:

1. Place the cooking pot in the Ninja Foodi Grill main unit.
2. In a mixing bowl, mix flour, baking soda, sugar, baking powder, and salt.
3. Add mashed bananas and vanilla and mix until well combined.
4. Pour batter into the greased loaf pan.
5. Press Bake mode, set the temperature to 350°F, and set time to 40 minutes. Press Start.
6. Once a unit is preheated then place the loaf pan in the cooking pot.
7. Cover with lid and cook for 40 minutes.

Nutrition:

- Calories: 181
- Fat: 3 g
- Sodium: 4 mg
- Carbs: 35 g
- Fiber: 1 g
- Sugar: 21 g
- Protein: 1 g

3. Banana Oat Muffins

Preparation time: 10 minutes
Cooking time: 20 minutes
Serving: 12
Ingredients:

- 1 egg
- 1 cup banana, mashed
- 2 1/4 cups old-fashioned oats
- 1/2 tsp. cinnamon
- 1 tsp. baking powder
- 1 tsp. vanilla
- 1/4 cup honey
- 3/4 cup milk
- 1/4 tsp. salt

Directions:

1. Place the cooking pot in the Ninja Foodi Grill main unit.
2. In a bowl, mix oats, cinnamon, baking powder, and salt and set aside.
3. In a separate bowl, whisk the egg with honey, vanilla, milk, and a mashed banana.
4. Add oat mixture into the egg mixture and mix until well combined.
5. Pour oat mixture into the greased silicone muffin molds.
6. Press Bake mode, set the temperature to 350°F and set time to 20 minutes. Press Start.
7. Once a unit is preheated then place muffin molds in the cooking pot.
8. Cover with lid and cook for 20 minutes.

Nutrition:

- Calories: 103
- Fat: 1.8 g
- Sodium: 64 mg
- Carbs: 19.9 g
- Fiber: 1.9 g
- Sugar: 8.5 g
- Protein: 3 g

4. Delicious Berry Oatmeal

Preparation time: 10 minutes
Cooking time: 20 minutes
Serving: 4
Ingredients:

- 1 egg
- 2 cups old-fashioned oats
- 1/2 cup strawberries, sliced
- 1/4 cup vanilla
- 1/4 cup maple syrup
- 1 1/2 cups milk
- 1 cup blueberries
- 1/2 cup blackberries
- 1 1/2 tsp. baking powder
- 1/2 tsp. salt

Directions:

1. Place the cooking pot in the Ninja Foodi Grill main unit.
2. In a bowl, mix oats, salt, and baking powder.
3. Add egg, vanilla, maple syrup, and milk and stir well. Add berries and stir well.
4. Pour the mixture into the greased baking dish.
5. Press Bake mode, set the temperature to 375°F and set time to 20 minutes. Press Start.
6. Once a unit is preheated then place the baking dish in the cooking pot.
7. Cover with lid and cook for 20 minutes.

Nutrition:

- Calories: 461
- Fat: 8.4 g
- Sodium: 353 mg
- Carbs: 80.7 g
- Fiber: 10.1 g
- Sugar: 23.4 g
- Protein: 15 g

5. Greek Egg Muffins

Preparation time: 10 minutes
Cooking time: 20 minutes
Serving: 12
Ingredients:

- 8 eggs
- 1 cup spinach, chopped
- 1/3 cup Feta cheese, crumbled
- 1/2 cup sun-dried tomatoes, sliced
- 1 tbsp. basil leaves, chopped
- 1/4 cup milk
- 1/2 onion, diced
- Pepper to taste
- Salt to taste

Directions:

1. Place the cooking pot in the Ninja Foodi Grill main unit.
2. In a bowl, whisk eggs with milk, pepper, and salt. Add remaining ingredients and stir well.
3. Pour egg mixture into the greased silicone muffin molds.
4. Press Bake mode, set the temperature to 350°F and set time to 20 minutes. Press Start.
5. Once a unit is preheated then place muffin molds in the cooking pot.
6. Cover with lid and cook for 20 minutes.

Nutrition:

- Calories: 59
- Fat: 3.9 g
- Sodium: 104 mg
- Carbs: 1.5 g
- Fiber: 0.3 g
- Sugar: 1 g
- Protein: 4.7 g

6. Breakfast Skewers

Preparation time: 15 minutes
Cooking time: 8 minutes
Serving: 4
Ingredients:

- 1 package (7 oz.) cooked sausage links, halved
- 1 can (20 oz.) pineapple chunks, drained
- 10 medium fresh mushrooms
- 2 tbsp. butter, melted
- Maple syrup to taste

Directions:

1. Toss sausages, pineapple, and mushrooms with butter and maple syrup in a bowl.
2. Thread these ingredients on the wooden skewers.
3. Select the "Grill" Mode, set the temperature to MED.
4. Use the arrow keys to set the cooking time to 8 minutes.
5. Press the START/STOP button to initiate preheating.
6. Once preheated, place the skewers in the Ninja Foodi Grill.
7. Cover the hood and allow the grill to cook.
8. Flip the skewers once cooked halfway through.
9. Serve warm.

Nutrition:

- Calories: 246
- Fat: 20 g
- Sodium: 114 mg
- Carbs: 13 g
- Fiber: 1 g
- Sugar: 10 g
- Protein: 7 g

7. Campfire Hash

Preparation time: 10 minutes.
Cooking time: 31 minutes.
Serving: 4
Ingredients:

- 1 large onion, chopped
- 2 tbsp. canola oil
- 2 garlic cloves, minced
- 4 large potatoes, peeled and cubed
- 1 lb. smoked kielbasa sausage, halved and sliced
- 1 can (4 oz.) green chiles, chopped
- 1 can (15- 1/4 oz.) whole kernel corn, drained

Directions:

1. Sauté the onion with canola oil in a skillet for 5 minutes.
2. Stir in garlic and sauté for 1 minute then transfer to a baking pan.
3. Toss in potatoes, kielbasa, chiles, and corn, and then mix well.
4. Select the "Bake" Mode, set the temperature to 400°F.
5. Use the arrow keys to set the cooking time to 20 minutes.
6. Press the START/STOP button to initiate preheating.
7. Once preheated, place the baking pan in the Ninja Foodi Grill.
8. Cover the hood and allow the grill to cook.
9. Serve warm.

Nutrition:

- Calories: 535
- Fat: 26 g
- Sodium: 1097 g
- Carbs: 46 g
- Fiber: 4 g
- Sugar: 8 g
- Protein: 17 g

8. Grilled Honeydew

Preparation time: 15 minutes
Cooking time: 6 minutes
Serving: 4
Ingredients:

- 1/4 cup peach preserves
- 1 tbsp. lemon juice
- 1 tbsp. crystallized ginger, chopped
- 2 tsp. lemon zest, grated
- 1/8 tsp. ground cloves
- 1 medium honeydew melon, cut into cubes

Directions:

1. Mix peach preserves with lemon juice, ginger, lemon zest, and cloves in a bowl.
2. Thread the honeydew melon on the wooden skewers.
3. Brush the prepared glaze over the skewers liberally.
4. Select the "Grill" Mode, set the temperature to MED.
5. Use the arrow keys to set the cooking time to 6 minutes.
6. Press the START/STOP button to initiate preheating.
7. Once preheated, place the skewers in the Ninja Foodi Grill.
8. Cover the hood and allow the grill to cook.
9. Flip the skewers once cooked halfway through.
10. Serve.

Nutrition:

- Calories: 101
- Fat: 0 g
- Sodium: 18 mg
- Carbs: 26 g
- Fiber: 3.6 g
- Sugar: 6 g
- Protein: 1 g

9. Zesty Grilled Ham

Preparation time: 15 minutes.
Cooking time: 10 minutes
Serving: 4
Ingredients:

- 1/3 cup packed brown sugar
- 2 tbsp. prepared horseradish
- 4 tsp. lemon juice
- 1 (1 lb.) fully cooked bone-in ham steak

Directions:

1. Boil brown sugar, lemon juice, and horseradish in a small saucepan.
2. Soak the ham slices in this mixture and coat well.
3. Select the "Grill" Mode, set the temperature to MED.
4. Press the START/STOP button to initiate preheating.
5. Once preheated, place the ham in the Ninja Foodi grill.
6. Cover the hood and allow the grill to cook.
7. Serve warm.

Nutrition:

- Calories: 180
- Fat: 5 g
- Sodium: 845 mg
- Carbs: 20 g
- Fiber: 0 g
- Sugar: 3 g
- Protein: 14 g

10. Ninja Foodi Breakfast Sausages

Preparation time: 10 minutes
Cooking time: 20 minutes
Serving: 6
Ingredients:

- 2 tsp. chili flakes
- 2 tsp. dried thyme
- 1 tsp. cayenne
- 4 tsp. tabasco
- 3 lb. ground sausage
- 1 tsp. paprika
- 4 tsp. brown sugar
- 2 tsp. onion powder
- 6 tsp. garlic, minced
- Salt and black pepper, to taste

Directions:

1. Install grill grate in the unit and close hood. Select GRILL, set temperature to HIGH, and set time to 20 minutes for medium-cooked burgers. Select START/STOP to begin preheating.
2. Meanwhile, add ground sausage, tabasco sauce, herbs, and spices in a large bowl. Mix well.
3. Make sausage-shaped patties out of the mixture and set them aside.
4. When the unit beeps to signify it has preheated, and shown Message "Add Food" place patties on the grill grate, gently pressing them down to maximize grill marks.
5. Flip halfway through and take out the sausages.
6. Serve and enjoy!

Nutrition:

- Calories: 787
- Fat: 64.5 g
- Sat fat: 20.7 g
- Carbs: 4.2 g
- Fiber: 0.5 g
- Sugar: 2.4 g
- Protein: 44.5 g

11. Ninja Foodi Swiss-Cheese Sandwiches

Preparation time: 10 minutes
Cooking time: 18 minutes
Serving: 4
Ingredients:

- 6 tbsp. half and half cream
- 2 eggs
- 3/4 cup Swiss cheese, sliced
- 1 tsp. powdered sugar
- 2 tsp. butter, melted
- 4 bread slices
- 1/2 tsp. vanilla extract
- 1/4 lb. deli turkey, sliced
- 1/4 lb. deli ham, sliced

Directions:

1. Insert grill grate in the unit and close hood. Select GRILL, set temperature to MED, and set time to 18 minutes. Select START/STOP to begin preheating.
2. In a separate bowl, combine half and half cream, eggs, butter, and vanilla essence. Mix thoroughly.
3. Layer ham, turkey, and Swiss cheese slices between 2 slices of bread.
4. Place the remaining bread slices on top and dip them in the egg mixture.
5. When the unit has beeps to signify it has preheated, and the shown message "Add Food" place the sandwich to the grill grate. Close hood and grill for 18 minutes.
6. After 9 minutes, flip the sandwich, then close the hood and continue cooking for 9 more minutes.
7. Dish out and top with powdered sugar.
8. Serve and enjoy!

Nutrition:

- Calories: 260 Fat: 15.9 g
- Sat fat: 8 g Carbs: 10.8 g
- Fiber: 0.7 g Sugar: 2.7 g Protein: 18.1 g

12. Ninja Foodi Bacon Bombs

Preparation time: 5 minutes
Cooking time: 7 minutes
Serving: 2
Ingredients:

- 2 eggs, lightly beaten
- 1 tbsp. cream cheese, softened
- 1/2 cup whole-wheat pizza dough, freshly prepared
- 2 bacon slices, crisped and crumbled
- 1/2 tbsp. fresh chives, chopped

Directions:

1. Insert grill grate in the unit and close hood. Select BAKE, set temperature to 350°F, and set time to 6 minutes. Select START/STOP to begin preheating.
2. In the meantime, crack eggs into a nonstick pan and stir-fry for 1 minute.
3. Combine the chives, bacon, and cream cheese in a mixing bowl. Set aside after thoroughly stirring.
4. Cut the pizza dough in half and roll each half into a round.
5. Fill the dough pieces with the bacon mixture and bind the edges with water.
6. When the unit beeps to signify it has preheated and Grill shows "Add Food," place the dough pieces in it and bake for about 6 minutes.
7. Take out, serve and enjoy!

Nutrition:

- Calories: 216
- Fat: 14.2 g
- Sat fat:5.6 g
- Carbs: 6.8 g
- Fiber: 1 g
- Sugar: 1.1 g
- Protein: 14.5 g

13. Ninja Foodi Bread and Bacon Cups

Preparation time: 12 minutes
Cooking time: 10 minutes
Serving: 4
Ingredients:

- 4 bread slices
- 8 tomato slices
- 4 eggs
- 1/4 tsp. balsamic vinegar
- 2 bacon slices, chopped
- 2 tbsp. shredded mozzarella cheese
- 1/4 tsp. maple syrup
- 1/2 tbsp. fresh parsley, chopped
- Salt and black pepper, to taste
- Butter to taste

Directions:

1. Arrange the bread slices in ramekins that have been lightly buttered and topped with tomato and bacon strips.
2. Add cheese, eggs, and maple syrup to the top of the mixture.
3. Drizzle with vinegar and season with salt, pepper, and parsley.
4. In the meantime, place the "Crisper Basket" in the Ninja Foodi Grill's cooking pot and close the hood.
5. Press the "AIR CRISP" button, then set the temperature to 320°F and the timer to 10 minutes. To begin preheating, press START/STOP. When the Ninja Foodi Grill says "Add Food," place the ramekins in the "Crisper Basket." Remove from the oven after around 10 minutes of cooking. Finally, serve and enjoy!

Nutrition:

- Calories: 185 Fat: 11.2 g
- Sat fat:4.2 g Carbs:7 g Fiber:0.6 g
- Sugar: 1.8 g Protein: 14 g

14. Ninja Foodi Breakfast Frittata

Preparation time: 15 minutes
Cooking time: 10 minutes
Serving: 6
Ingredients:

- 1 cup grated parmesan cheese, divided
- 2 bacon slices, chopped
- 2 tbsp. olive oil
- 12 cherry tomatoes, halved
- 6 eggs
- 12 fresh mushrooms, sliced
- Salt and black pepper, to taste

Directions:

1. Insert grill grate in the unit and close hood. Select GRILL, set temperature to MED, and set time to 10 minutes. Select START/STOP to begin preheating.
2. Meanwhile, add tomatoes, bacon, mushrooms, black pepper, and salt in a large bowl. Mix well.
3. Take another bowl and beat eggs and cheese in it.
4. When the unit beeps to signify it has preheated and Ninja Foodi Grill shows "Add Food," place the bacon mixture and top with eggs mixture on the grill grate. Close hood and cook for 5 minutes.
5. After 5 minutes, flip it, then close the hood and continue cooking for 5 more minutes.
6. Dish out and serve hot.

Nutrition:

- Calories: 204
- Fat: 13.3 g
- Sat fat: 3.6 g
- Carbs: 11.4 g
- Fiber: 3.3 g
- Sugar: 7.4 g
- Protein: 12.7 g

15. Ninja Foodi Cinnamon Buttered Toasts

Preparation time: 10 minutes
Cooking time: 5 minutes
Serving: 6
Ingredients:

- 1/2 cup sugar
- 1 1/2 tsp. vanilla extract
- 1/2 cup salted butter, softened
- 1 1/2 tsp. ground cinnamon
- 1/4 tsp. freshly ground black pepper
- 12 whole-wheat bread slices

Directions:

1. In a large mixing bowl, combine the vanilla, sugar, black pepper, cinnamon, and butter. Mix until you have a smooth batter.
2. Place the bread slices on top of the mixture and set them aside.
3. Meanwhile, in a Ninja Foodi Grill, place the "Crisper Basket" and close the lid.
4. Select "AIR CRISP," set the temperature to 400°F and the timer to 5 minutes.
5. To begin preheating, press START/STOP.
6. Place the bread slices in the "Crisper Basket" and cook for 5 minutes when the Ninja Foodi Grill says "Add Food."
7. Remove from the unit and serve.

Nutrition:

- Calories: 353
- Fat: 17.3 g
- Sat fat: 10.2 g
- Carbs: 42.1 g
- Fiber: 5 g
- Sugar: 20.3 g
- Protein: 7.5 g

16. The Broccoli and Maple Mix

Preparation time: 5 to 10 minutes
Cooking time: 10 minutes
Serving: 4
Ingredients:

- 2 heads broccoli, cut into florets
- 4 tbsp. soy sauce
- 2 tsp. maple syrup
- 4 tbsp. balsamic vinegar
- 2 tsp. canola oil
- Red pepper flakes and sesame seeds for garnish

Directions:

1. Take a shallow mixing bowl and add vinegar, soy sauce, oil, maple syrup.
2. Whisk the whole mixture thoroughly.
3. Add broccoli to the mix.
4. Keep it aside. Set your Ninja Foodi Grill to GRILL mode at MAX heat.
5. Set the timer to 10 minutes.
6. Once you hear the beep, add prepared broccoli over Grill Grate.
7. Cook for 10 minutes.
8. Serve and enjoy!

Nutrition:

- Calories: 141
- Fat: 7 g
- Fat: 1 g
- Carbs: 14 g
- Fiber: 4 g
- Sodium: 853 mg
- Protein: 4 g

17. Sausage with Eggs

Preparation time: 15 minutes
Cooking time: 10 minutes
Serving: 4
Ingredients:

- 4 sausage links
- 2 cups kale, chopped
- 1 sweet yellow onion, chopped
- 4 eggs
- 1 cup mushrooms
- 1/8 tsp. olive oil

Directions:

1. Preheat the Ninja Foodi Grill on the "Grill Mode" at LOW-temperature settings.
2. When the grill is preheated, open its hood and place the sausages on the Ninja grill.
3. Cover the grill's hood and grill for 2 minutes.
4. Flip the sausages and continue grilling for another 3 minutes
5. Now spread olive oil, the onion, mushrooms, sausages, and kale in an iron skillet.
6. Crack the eggs in between the sausages.
7. BAKE this mixture for 5 minutes in the grill at 350°F.
8. Serve warm and fresh.

Nutrition:

- Calories: 212
- Fat: 12 g
- Sodium: 321 mg
- Carbs: 14.6 g
- Fiber: 4 g
- Sugar: 8 g
- Protein: 17 g

18. Veggie Packed Egg Muffin

Preparation time: 5 to 10 minutes
Cooking time: 7 minutes
Serving: 4
Ingredients:

- 4 whole eggs
- 2 tbsp. almond flour
- 1 tsp. butter
- 1 zucchini, grated
- 1/2 tsp. salt

Directions:

1. Add eggs, almond flour, zucchini, and salt into a mixing bowl.
2. Mix them well.
3. Grease muffin molds with butter.
4. Adds zucchini mixture to them.
5. Arrange muffin tins in your Ninja Foodi Grill and lock the lid.
6. Cook on "AIR CRISP" mode for 7 minutes at 375°F.

Nutrition:

- Calories: 94
- Fat: 8 g
- Carbs: 2 g
- Fiber: 0.5 g
- Sodium: 209 mg
- Protein: 7 g

19. Bacon-Herb Grit

Preparation time: 15 minutes
Cooking time: 10 minutes
Serving: 4
Ingredients:

- 2 tsp. fresh parsley, chopped
- 1/2 tsp. garlic powder
- 1/2 tsp. black pepper
- 3 bacon slices, cooked and crumbled
- 1/2 cup cheddar cheese, shredded
- 4 cups instant grits
- Cooking spray

Directions:

1. Start by mixing the first seven ingredients in a suitable bowl.
2. Spread this mixture in a 10-inch baking pan and refrigerate for 1 hour.
3. Flip the pan on a plate and cut the grits mixture into 4 triangles.
4. Preheat the Ninja Foodi Grill on the "Grill Mode" at MEDIUM-temperature settings.
5. When the grill is preheated, open its hood and place the grit slices in it.
6. Cover the grill's hood and grill for 5 minutes per side.
7. Serve warm.

Nutrition:

- Calories: 197
- Fat: 15 g
- Sodium: 548 mg
- Carbs: 59 g
- Fiber: 4 g
- Sugar: 1 g
- Protein: 7.9 g

20. Cinnamon Oatmeal

Preparation time: 10 minutes
Cooking time: 30 minutes
Serving: 8
Ingredients:

- 2 eggs
- 3 cups rolled oats
- 1/4 cup butter, melted
- 1/2 cup maple syrup
- 1 1/2 cups unsweetened almond milk
- 1 tsp. ground cinnamon
- 1 tsp. vanilla
- 1 1/2 tsp. baking powder
- Pinch of salt

Directions:

1. Place the cooking pot in the Ninja Foodi Grill main unit.
2. In a bowl, whisk eggs with milk, cinnamon, vanilla, baking powder, butter, maple syrup, and salt. Add oats and stir well.
3. Pour oat mixture into the greased baking pan.
4. Press Bake mode, set the temperature to 350°F and set time to 30 minutes. Press Start.
5. Once Ninja Foodi Grill is preheated then place your own baking pan in the cooking pot.
6. Cover with lid and cook for 30 minutes.

Nutrition:

- Calories: 245
- Fat: 9.5 g
- Sodium: 114 mg
- Carbs: 35.2 g
- Fiber: 3.5 g
- Sugar: 12.2 g
- Protein: 5.7 g

21. Spinach Tater Tot Casserole

Preparation time: 10 minutes
Cooking time: 40 minutes
Serving: 8
Ingredients:

- 8 eggs
- 15 oz. frozen tater tots
- 1 1/2 cup cheddar cheese, shredded
- 4 oz. fresh spinach, chopped and sautéed
- 1 cup roasted red peppers, chopped
- Pepper to taste
- Salt to taste

Directions:

1. Place the cooking pot in the Ninja Foodi Grill main unit.
2. In a bowl, whisk eggs with pepper and salt. Add cheese, roasted peppers, and spinach, and stir well.
3. Place the tater tots into the greased baking dish. Pour egg mixture over tater tots.
4. Press Bake mode, set the temperature to 350°F and set time to 40 minutes. Press START.
5. Once a unit is preheated then place the baking dish in the cooking pot.
6. Cover with lid and cook for 40 minutes.

Nutrition:

- Calories: 254
- Fat: 16 g
- Sodium: 680 mg
- Carbs: 15 g
- Fiber: 1 g
- Sugar: 680 g
- Protein: 12 g

22. Ninja Foodi Bean

Preparation time: 5 minutes
Cooking time: 10 minutes
Serving: 4
Ingredients:

- Flaky sea salt to taste
- Pinch of pepper
- 1 lemon, juiced
- 2 tbsp. oils
- 1 lb. green bean, trimmed
- Pepper flakes to taste

Directions:

1. Take a medium bowl and add the green bean.
2. Mix and stir well.
3. Select the GRILL mode, adjust the temperature to MAX and time to 10minutes. Press START/STOP to preheat.
4. Wait until you hear a beep. Transfer beans to the grill grate, cook for 8 to 10 minutes.
5. Toss well to ensure that all sides are cooked evenly.
6. Squeeze a bit of lemon juice and oil on the top.
7. Season with salt, pepper, and pepper flakes according to your taste.
8. Enjoy!

Nutrition:

- Calories: 100
- Carbs: 10 g
- Protein: 2 g
- Fat: 7 g
- Sodium: 30 mg
- Fiber: 4 g

23. Kale and Sausage Delight

Preparation time: 10 minutes
Cooking time: 10 minutes
Serving: 4
Ingredients:

- Olive oil as needed
- 1 cup mushrooms
- 2 cups kale, fine chopped
- 4 sausage links
- 4 medium eggs
- 1 medium yellow onion, sweet

Directions:

1. Open the lid of your Ninja Foodi Grill and arrange the Grill Grate.
2. Pre-heat your Ninja Foodi Grill to HIGH and set the timer to 5 minutes with GRILL mode.
3. Once you hear the beeping sound, arrange sausages over the grill grate.
4. Cook for 2 minutes, flip and cook for 3 minutes more.
5. Take a baking pan and spread out the kale, onion, mushroom, sausage, and crack an egg on top. Cook on BAKE mode at 350°F for about 5 minutes more.
6. Serve and enjoy!

Nutrition:

- Calories: 236
- Carbs: 17 g
- Protein: 18 g
- Fat: 12 g
- Sodium: 369 mg
- Fiber: 4 g

24. Butternut Squash With Italian Herbs

Preparation time: 5 to 10 minutes
Cooking time: 16 minutes
Serving: 4
Ingredients:

- 1 medium butternut squash, peeled, seeded, and cut into 1/2 inch slices
- 1 tsp. dried thyme
- 1 tbsp. olive oil
- 1 1/2 tsp. oregano, dried
- 1/4 tsp. black pepper
- 1/2 tsp. salt

Directions:

1. Add all the ingredients into a mixing bowl and mix it.
2. Pre-heat your Ninja Foodi by pressing the "GRILL" option and setting it to "MEDIUM.".
3. Set the timer to 16 minutes.
4. Allow it to pre-heat until you hear a beep.
5. Arrange squash slices over the grill grate.
6. Cook for 8 minutes.
7. Flip them and cook for 8 minutes more.
8. Serve and enjoy!

Nutrition:

- Calories: 238
- Carbs: 36 g
- Protein: 158 g
- Fat: 12 g
- Sodium: 128 mg
- Fiber: 3 g

25. Stuffed up Bacon and Pepper

Preparation time: 10 minutes
Cooking time: 15 minutes
Serving: 4
Ingredients:

- Chopped parsley, for garnish
- Salt and pepper to taste
- 4 whole large eggs
- 4 bell peppers, seeded and tops removed
- 4 slices bacon, cooked and chopped
- 1 cup cheddar cheese, shredded

Directions:

1. Take the bell pepper and divide the cheese and bacon evenly between them.
2. Crack eggs into each of the bell pepper.
3. Season the bell pepper with salt and pepper.
4. Pre-heat your Ninja Food Grill in AIR CRISP mode with a temperature of 390°F.
5. Set timer to 15 minutes.
6. Once you hear the beep, transfer the bell pepper to the cooking basket.
7. Transfer your prepared pepper to Ninja Foodi Grill and cook for 10 to 15 minutes until the eggs are cooked, and the yolks are just slightly runny.

Nutrition:

- Calories: 326
- Fat: 23 g
- Carbs: 10 g
- Fiber: 2 g
- Sodium: 781 mg
- Protein: 22 g

26. Epic Breakfast Burrito

Preparation time: 5 to 10 minutes
Cooking time: 30 minutes
Serving: 4
Ingredients:

- 12 tortillas
- Salt and pepper to taste
- 2 cups potatoes, diced
- 3 cups cheddar cheese, shredded
- 10 whole eggs, beaten
- 1 lb. breakfast sausage
- 1 tsp. olive oil

Directions:

1. Pour olive oil into a pan over medium heat.
2. Cook potatoes and sausage for 7 to 10 minutes, stirring frequently.
3. Spread this mixture on the bottom of the Ninja Foodi Grill pot.
4. Season with salt and pepper.
5. Pour the eggs and cheese on top.
6. Select BAKE setting. Cook at 325°F for 20 minutes.
7. Top the tortilla with the cooked mixture and roll.
8. Sprinkle cheese on the top side. Add a Crisper basket to Ninja Foodi Grill.
9. AIR CRISP the Burritos for 10 minutes at 375°F.
10. Serve and enjoy!

Nutrition:

- Calories: 400
- Fat: 20 g
- Carbs: 36 g
- Fiber: 5 g
- Sodium: 675 mg
- Protein: 22 g

27. Energetic Bagel Platter

Preparation time: 5 to 10 minutes
Cooking time: 8 minutes
Serving: 4
Ingredients:

- 4 bagels, halved
- 2 tbsp. coconut flakes
- 1 cup fine sugar
- 2 tbsp. black coffee prepared and cooled down
- 1/4 cup of coconut milk

Directions:

1. Take your Ninja Foodi Grill and open the lid.
2. Arrange grill grate and close top.
3. Pre-heat Ninja Foodi by pressing the "GRILL" option and setting it to "MEDIUM.".
4. Set the timer to 8 minutes.
5. Let it pre-heat until you hear a beep.
6. Arrange bagels over the grill grate and lock lid.
7. Cook for 2 minutes.
8. Flip bagels and cook for 2 minutes more.
9. Repeat the same procedure to grill the remaining Bagels.
10. Take a mixing bowl and mix the remaining Ingredients Pour the sauce over grilled bagels
11. Serve and enjoy!

Nutrition:

- Calories: 300
- Carbs: 42 g
- Protein: 18 g
- Fat: 23 g
- Sodium: 340 mg
- Fiber: 4 g

28. Morning Frittata

Preparation time: 10 minutes
Cooking time: 10 minutes
Serving: 4
Ingredients:

- 4 large eggs
- 4 cups cremini mushrooms, sliced
- 1/2 bell pepper, seeded and diced
- 1/2 cup shredded cheddar cheese
- 1/2 onion, chopped
- 1/4 cup whole milk
- Salt and pepper to taste

Directions:

1. Add eggs and milk into a medium-sized bowl.
2. Whisk it and then season with salt and pepper.
3. Then add bell pepper, onion, mushroom, cheese. Mix them well.
4. Pre-heat Ninja Foodi Grill by pressing the "BAKE" option and setting it to "400°F."
5. Set the timer to 10 minutes.
6. Let it pre-heat until you hear a beep.
7. Pour Egg Mixture in your bake pan, spread well.
8. Transfer to Grill and lock lid.
9. Bake for 10 minutes until lightly golden.
10. Serve and enjoy!

Nutrition:

- Calories: 153
- Fat: 10 g
- Carbs: 5 g
- Fiber: 1 g
- Sodium: 177 mg
- Protein: 11 g

29. Breakfast Potato Casserole

Preparation time: 10 minutes
Cooking time: 35 minutes
Serving: 10
Ingredients:

- 7 eggs
- 8 oz. cheddar cheese, grated
- 1 lb. sausage, cooked
- 20 oz. frozen hash browns, diced
- 1/2 cup unsweetened almond milk
- 1 onion, chopped and sautéed
- Pepper to taste
- Salt to taste

Directions:

1. Place the cooking pot in the Ninja Foodi Grill main unit.
2. In a bowl, whisk eggs with milk, pepper, and salt. Add remaining ingredients and mix well.
3. Pour egg mixture into the greased baking dish.
4. Press Bake mode, set the temperature to 350°F and set time to 35 minutes. Press Start.
5. Once a unit is preheated then place the baking dish in the cooking pot.
6. Cover with lid and cook for 35 minutes.

Nutrition:

- Calories: 446 Fat: 30.7 g
- Sodium: 743 mg
- Carbs: 21.6 g
- Fiber: 2.1 g
- Sugar: 1.7 g
- Protein: 20.2 g

30. Avocado Eggs

Preparation time: 15 minutes
Cooking time: 8 minutes
Serving: 2
Ingredients:

- 2 eggs
- 1 ripe avocado
- 1 pinch of barbecue rub
- Salt and pepper, to taste

Directions:

1. Slice the avocado in half and remove its pit.
2. Remove some flesh from the center.
3. Drizzle barbecue rub, salt, and black pepper on top.
4. Preheat the Ninja Foodi Grill on the "Grill Mode" at LOW-temperature settings.
5. When the grill is preheated, open its hood and place the avocados in it with their skin-side down.
6. Cover the grill's hood and grill for 8 minutes.
7. Flip the avocados once grilled halfway through.
8. Crack an egg into each half of the avocado.
9. Serve.

Nutrition:

- Calories: 322
- Fat: 12 g
- Sodium: 202 mg
- Carbs: 14.6 g
- Fiber: 4 g
- Sugar: 8 g
- Protein: 17.3 g

CHAPTER 4:

Snacks And Appetizers

31. Fajita Skewers

Preparation time: 10 minutes
Cooking time: 14 minutes
Serving: 8
Ingredients:

- 1 lb. sirloin steak, cubed
- Olive oil, for drizzling
- 1 bunch scallions cut into large pieces
- 4 large bell peppers, cubed
- 1 pack tortillas, torn
- Salt to taste
- Black pepper grounded to taste

Directions:

1. Thread the steak, tortillas, scallions, and pepper on the skewers
2. Drizzle olive oil, salt, black pepper over the skewers
3. Pre-heat Ninja Foodi by pressing the "GRILL" option and setting it to "MED"
4. Once preheated, open the lid and place 4 skewers on the grill
5. Cover the lid and grill for 7 minutes
6. Keep rotating skewers for every 2 minutes
7. Serve warm and enjoy!

Nutrition:

- Calories: 353
- Carbs: 11 g
- Fat: 7.5 g
- Protein: 13.1 g

32. Seared Tuna Salad

Preparation time: 10 minutes
Cooking time: 6 minutes
Serving: 4
Ingredients:

- 1/2 lb. ahi tuna, cut into four strips
- 2 tbsp. sesame oil
- 1(10 oz.) bag baby greens
- 2 tbsp. rice wine vinegar
- 6 tbsp. extra-virgin olive oil
- 1/2 English cucumber, sliced
- 1/4 tsp. sea salt
- 1/2 tsp. ground black pepper

Directions:

1. Supplement the flame broil mesh and close the hood
2. Pre-heat Ninja Foodi by pressing the "GRILL" option and setting it to "MAX" and timer to 6 minutes
3. Take a small bowl, whisk together the rice vinegar, salt, and pepper
4. Slowly pour in the oil while whisking until vinaigrette is fully combined
5. Season the fish with salt and pepper, sprinkle with the sesame oil
6. Once its pre-heat until you hear a beep
7. Arrange the shrimp over the grill grate lock lid and cook for 6 minutes
8. Do not flip during cooking
9. Once cooked completely, top salad with tuna strip
10. Drizzle the vinaigrette over the top
11. Serve immediately and enjoy!

Nutrition:

- Calories: 427
- Carbs: 5 g
- Fat: 30 g.
- Protein: 36 g

33. Crispy Potato Cubes

Preparation time: 10 minutes
Cooking time: 20 minutes
Serving: 4
Ingredients:

- 1 lb. potato, peeled
- 1 tbsp. olive oil
- 1 tsp. dried dill
- 1 tsp. dried oregano
- 1/4 tsp. chili flakes

Directions:

1. Pre-heat Ninja Foodi by squeezing the "AIR CRISP" alternative and setting it to "400°F" and timer to 20 minutes
2. Let it pre-heat until you hear a beep
3. Cut potatoes into cubes
4. Sprinkle potato cubes with dill, olive oil, oregano, and chili flakes
5. Transfer to Foodi Grill and cook for 15 minutes
6. Stir while cooking, once they are crunchy
7. Serve and enjoy!

Nutrition:

- Calories: 119
- Carbs: 20 g
- Fat: 4 g.
- Protein: 12 g

34. Lemon-Garlic Shrimp Caesar Salad

Preparation time: 10 minutes
Cooking time: 5 minutes
Serving: 4
Ingredients:

- 1 lb. fresh jumbo shrimp
- 2 heads romaine lettuce, chopped
- 3/4 cup Caesar dressing
- 1/2 cup parmesan cheese, grated
- 1/2 lemon juice
- 3 garlic cloves, minced
- Sea salt to taste
- Black pepper grounded to taste

Directions:

1. Addition the flame broils mesh and close the hood. Pre-heat Ninja Foodi by pressing the "GRILL" option and setting it to "MAX" and timer to 5 minutes
2. Take a large bowl; toss the shrimp with the lemon juice, garlic, salt, and pepper
3. Let it marinate while the grill is preheating
4. Once its pre-heat until you hear a beep
5. Arrange the shrimp over the grill grate lock lid and cook for 5 minutes
6. Toss the romaine lettuce with the Caesar dressing
7. Once cooked completely, remove the shrimp from the grill
8. Sprinkle with parmesan cheese
9. Serve and enjoy!

Nutrition:

- Calories: 279
- Carbs: 17 g
- Fat: 11 g
- Protein: 30 g

35. Simple Crispy Brussels

Preparation time: 10 minutes
Cooking time: 12 minutes
Serving: 4
Ingredients:

- 1 lb. Brussels sprouts halved
- 2 tbsp. olive oil, extra virgin
- 1/2 tsp. ground black pepper
- 1 tsp. salt
- 6 slices bacon, chopped

Directions:

1. Take a mixing bowl and add Brussels, olive oil, salt, pepper, and bacon
2. Pre-heat Ninja Foodi by squeezing the "AIR CRISP" alternative and setting it to 390°F and clock to 12 minutes
3. Let it pre-heat until you hear a beep
4. Arrange Brussels over basket and lock lid, cook for 6 minutes, shake and cook for 6 minutes more
5. Serve and enjoy!

Nutrition:

- Calories: 279
- Carbs: 12 g
- Fat: 18 g
- Protein: 14 g

36. Appetizer of Chicken Wings with Cajun Eggplant

Preparation time: 5 to 10 minutes
Cooking time: 10 minutes
Serving: 8
Ingredients:

- 3 lb. chicken wings
- 2 small eggplants cut into slices
- 1/4 cup olive oil
- 2 tbsp. lime juice
- 3 tsp. Cajun seasoning

Directions:

1. Coat the eggplant slices with oil, lemon juices and Cajun seasoning add the chicken wings and combine well to coat
2. Arrange the grill grate and close the lid
3. Pre-heat Ninja Foodi by pressing the "GRILL" option and setting it to "MED" and timer to 10 minutes
4. Let it pre-heat until you hear a beep
5. Arrange the eggplant slices over the grill grate, lock a lid and cook for 5 minutes
6. Flip the chicken and close the lid, cook for 5 minutes more
7. Serve warm and enjoy!

Nutrition:

- Calories: 362
- Carbs: 16 g
- Fat: 11 g
- Protein: 8 g

37. Portobello and Pesto Sliders

Preparation time: 10 minutes
Cooking time: 8 minutes
Serving: 4
Ingredients:

- 8 small Portobello mushrooms, trimmed with gills removed
- 1 tomato, sliced
- 2 tbsp. canola oil
- 1/2 cup pesto
- 1/2 cup microgreens
- 2 tbsp. balsamic vinegar
- 8 slider buns

Directions:

1. Addition the flame broils mesh and close the hood
2. Pre-heat Ninja Foodi by pressing the "GRILL" option and setting it to "HIGH" and timer to 8 minutes
3. Brush the mushrooms with oil and balsamic vinegar
4. Once its pre-heat until you hear a beep
5. Arrange the mushrooms over the grill grate lock lid and cook for 8 minutes
6. Once cooked, remove the mushrooms from the grill and layer on the buns with tomato, pesto, and microgreens
7. Serve immediately and enjoy!

Nutrition:

- Calories: 373
- Carbs: 33 g
- Fat: 22 g
- Protein: 12 g

38. Healthy Onion Rings

Preparation time: 10 minutes
Cooking time: 10 minutes
Serving: 4
Ingredients:

- 1/4 tsp. salt
- 1 egg
- 3/4 cup milk
- 1 tbsp. baking powder
- 3/4 cup breadcrumbs
- 1 large onion
- 1 cup flour
- 1 tsp. paprika
- Cooking spray

Directions:

1. Pre-heat Ninja Foodi by squeezing the "AIR CRISP" alternative and setting it to "340°F" and timer to 10 minutes
2. Let it pre-heat until you hear a beep
3. Take a bowl and whisk the egg, milk, salt, flour, baking powder, paprika together
4. Slice the onion and separate it into rings
5. Grease your Ninja Foodi Grill with cooking spray
6. Then dip the onion rings into batter and coat with breadcrumbs
7. Arrange them in Ninja Foodi Grill Cooking Basket
8. Cook for 10 minutes
9. Serve and enjoy!

Nutrition:

- Calories: 450
- Carbs: 56 g
- Fat: 13 g.
- Protein: 30 g

39. Bacon Brussels Delight

Preparation time: 5 to 10 minutes
Cooking time: 12 minutes
Serving: 4
Ingredients:

- 6 slices bacon, chopped
- 1 lb. Brussels sprouts halved
- 1/2 tsp. black pepper
- 1 tbsp. sea salt
- 2 tbsp. olive oil, extra-virgin

Directions:

1. Take a mixing bowl and toss the Brussels sprouts, olive oil, bacon, salt, and black pepper
2. Arrange the crisping basket inside the pot
3. Pre-heat Ninja Foodi by squeezing the "AIR CRISP" setting at 390°F and timer to 12 minutes
4. Let it pre-heat until you hear a beep
5. Arrange the Brussels sprout mixture directly inside the basket
6. Close the top lid and cook for 6 minutes, then shake the basket
7. Close the top lid and cook for 6 minutes more
8. Serve warm and enjoy!

Nutrition:

- Calories: 279
- Carbs: 12.5 g
- Fat: 18.5 g
- Protein: 14.5 g

40. Honey Mustard Chicken Tenders

Preparation time: 5 minutes
Cooking time: 3 minutes
Serving: 4
Ingredients:

- 2 lb. chicken tenders
- 1/2 cup Dijon mustard
- 1/2 cup walnuts
- 2 tbsp. honey
- 2 tbsp. olive oil
- 1 tsp. black pepper, ground

Directions:

1. Grab a bowl, using a whisk mix the mustard, olive oil, honey, and pepper into it
2. Add the chicken and toss to coat
3. Grind the walnut in your food processor
4. Supplement the flame broil mesh and close the hood
5. Pre-heat Ninja Foodi by pressing the "GRILL" option and setting it to "HIGH" for 4 minutes
6. Toss the chicken tenders in the ground walnuts to coat them lightly
7. Grill the chicken tender for 3 minutes
8. Serve hot and enjoy!

Nutrition:

- Calories: 444
- Carbs: 26 g
- Fat: 20 g
- Protein: 6 g

41. Honey Asparagus

Preparation time: 10 minutes
Cooking time: 15 minutes
Serving: 4
Ingredients:

- 2 lb. asparagus, trimmed
- 1/2 tsp. pepper
- 1 tsp. salt
- 1/4 cup honey
- 2 tbsp. olive oil
- 4 tbsp. tarragon, minced

Directions:

1. Take a bowl and add asparagus, oil, salt, honey, pepper, tarragon, and toss well
2. Pre-heat Ninja Foodi by pressing the "GRILL" option and setting it to "MED" and timer to 8 minutes
3. Let it pre-heat until you hear a beep
4. Arrange asparagus over grill grate, lock lid and cook for 4 minutes, flip asparagus and cook for 4 minutes more
5. Serve and enjoy!

Nutrition:

- Calories: 240
- Carbs: 31 g
- Fat: 15 g
- Protein: 7 g

42. Pumpkin Fries

Preparation time: 10 minutes
Cooking time: 35 minutes
Serving: 2
Ingredients:

- 14 oz. pumpkin, peeled and cut into strips
- 2 tsp. olive oil
- 1/2 tsp. ground cinnamon
- 1/2 tsp. red chili powder
- 1/4 tsp. garlic salt
- Salt and freshly ground black pepper, to taste

Directions:

1. In a bowl, add all the ingredients and toss to coat well.
2. Arrange the greased "Crisper Basket" in the pot of Ninja Foodi Grill.
3. Close the Ninja Foodi Grill with lid and select "Air Crisp."
4. Set the temperature to 400°F to preheat.
5. Press "Start/Stop" to begin preheating.
6. When the display shows "Add Food" open the lid and arrange the fries in "Crisper Basket."
7. Close the Ninja Foodi Grill with a lid and set the time for 30 minutes.
8. Press "Start/Stop" to begin cooking.
9. When cooking time is completed, press "Start/Stop" to stop cooking and open the lid.
10. Serve warm.

Nutrition:

- Calories: 112
- Fat: 5.4 g
- Sat fat: 1 g
- Carbs: 17.1 g
- Fiber: 6.3 g
- Sugar: 6.7 g
- Protein: 2.3 g

43. Apple Chips

Preparation time: 10 minutes
Cooking time: 8 minutes
Serving: 2
Ingredients:

- 1 apple, peeled, cored, and thinly sliced
- 1 tbsp. sugar
- 1/2 tsp. ground cinnamon
- Pinch of ground cardamom
- Pinch of ground ginger
- Pinch of salt

Directions:

1. In a bowl, add all the ingredients and toss to coat well.
2. Arrange the greased "Crisper Basket" in the pot of Ninja Foodi Grill.
3. Close the Ninja Foodi Grill with a lid and select "Air Crisp."
4. Set the temperature to 390°F to preheat.
5. Press "Start/Stop" to begin preheating.
6. When the display shows "Add Food" open the lid and arrange the apple chips in "Crisper Basket."
7. Close the Ninja Foodi Grill with a lid and set the time for 6 minutes.
8. Press "Start/Stop" to begin cooking.
9. When cooking time is completed, press "Start/Stop" to stop cooking and open the lid.
10. Set the apple chips aside to cool before serving.

Nutrition:

- Calories: 83
- Fat: 0.2 g
- Sat fat: 0 g
- Carbs: 22 g
- Fiber: 3.1 g
- Sugar: 17.6 g
- Protein: 0.3 g

44. Cheddar Meatballs

Preparation time: 15 minutes
Cooking time: 14 minutes
Serving: 2
Ingredients:

- 1/2 lb. ground turkey
- 1 onion, chopped
- 1 tsp. garlic paste
- 2 tbsp. fresh basil, chopped
- 1 tsp. mustard
- 1 tsp. maple syrup
- 1 tbsp. Cheddar cheese, grated
- Salt and freshly ground black pepper, to taste

Directions:

1. In a bowl, add all ingredients and mix until well combined.
2. Make small equal-sized balls from the mixture.
3. Arrange the greased "Crisper Basket" in the pot of Ninja Foodi Grill.
4. Close the Ninja Foodi Grill with lid and select "Air Crisp."
5. Set the temperature to 390°F to preheat.
6. Press "Start/Stop" to begin preheating.
7. When the display shows "Add Food" open the lid and arrange the meatballs in "Crisper Basket."
8. Close the Ninja Foodi Grill with a lid and set the time for 14 minutes.
9. Press "Start/Stop" to begin cooking.
10. When cooking time is completed, press "Start/Stop" to stop cooking and open the lid.
11. Serve hot.

Nutrition:

- Calories: 277
- Fat: 14.2 g
- Sat fat: 2.8 g
- Carbs: 8.5 g
- Fiber: 1.5 g
- Sugar: 4.5 g
- Protein: 33.1 g

45. BBQ Chicken Wings

Preparation time: 15 minutes
Cooking time: 19 minutes
Serving: 4
Ingredients:

- 2 lb. chicken wings
- 1 tsp. olive oil
- 1 tsp. smoked paprika
- 1 tsp. garlic powder
- Salt and freshly ground black pepper, to taste
- 1/4 cup barbecue sauce

Directions:

1. Arrange the "Crisper Basket" in the pot of Ninja Foodi Grill.
2. Close the Ninja Foodi Grill with lid and select "Air Crisp."
3. Set the temperature to 360°F to preheat.
4. Press "Start/Stop" to begin preheating.
5. In a large bowl combine chicken wings, smoked paprika, garlic powder, oil, salt, and black pepper and mix well.
6. When the display shows "Add Food" open the lid and place the chicken wings in the "Crisper Basket" in a single layer.
7. Close the Ninja Foodi Grill with lid and select "Air Crisp."
8. Set the temperature to 360°F for 19 minutes.
9. Press "Start/Stop" to begin cooking.
10. After 12 minutes of cooking, flip the wings and coat with barbecue sauce evenly.
11. When cooking time is completed, press "Start/Stop" to stop cooking and open the lid.
12. Serve immediately.

Nutrition:

- Calories: 468 Fat: 18.1 g
- Sat fat: 4.8 g Carbs: 6.5 g
- Fiber: 0.4 g
- Sugar: 4.3 g
- Protein: 65.8 g

46. Chicken Nuggets

Preparation time: 20 minutes
Cooking time: 10 minutes
Serving: 5
Ingredients:

- 1/2 of zucchini, chopped roughly
- 1/2 of carrot, peeled and chopped roughly
- 14 oz. boneless, skinless chicken breasts, cut into chunks - 1/2 tbsp. mustard powder
- 1 tbsp. garlic powder
- 1 tbsp. onion powder
- Salt and ground black pepper, as required
- 1 cup all-purpose flour
- 2 tbsp. milk - 1 egg - 1 cup panko breadcrumbs

Directions:

1. In a food processor, add zucchini and carrot and pulse until chopped finely. Add the chicken, mustard powder, garlic powder, onion powder, salt, and black pepper and pulse until just combined. Make equal-sized nuggets from the mixture.
2. In a shallow dish, place the flour.
3. In a second shallow dish, beat the milk and egg.
4. In a third shallow dish, place the breadcrumbs.
5. Coat the nuggets with flour, then dip into the egg mixture, and finally, coat with the breadcrumbs.
6. Arrange the "Crisper Basket" in the pot of Ninja Foodi Ninja Foodi Grill with a lid and select "Air Crisp."Set the temperature to 390°F to preheat.
7. Press "Start/Stop" to begin preheating.
8. When the display shows "Add Food" open the lid and place the nuggets into the "Crisper Basket" in a single layer.
9. Close the Ninja Foodi Grill with a lid and set the time for 10 minutes. Press "Start/Stop" to begin cooking. When the cooking time is completed, press "Start/Stop" to stop cooking and open the lid. Serve warm.

Nutrition:

- Calories: 537Fat: 9 g
- Sat fat: 2.6 g Carbs: 26.7 g
- Fiber: 1.5 g Sugar: 2.1 g Protein: 28.4 g

47. Little Smokies

Preparation time: 15 minutes
Cooking time: 10 minutes
Serving: 8
Ingredients:

- 2/3 lb. bacon strips
- 14 oz. little smokies
- 1/3 cup brown sugar

Directions:

1. Cut the bacon strips into thirds across the width.
2. In a shallow dish, place the brown sugar.
3. Coat both sides of bacon strips with brown sugar.
4. Wrap each smokie with a bacon piece.
5. Then secure each wrapped smokie with a toothpick.
6. Arrange the "Crisper Basket" in the pot of Ninja Foodi Grill.
7. Close the Ninja Foodi Grill with lid and select "Air Crisp."
8. Set the temperature to 350°F to preheat.
9. Press "Start/Stop" to begin preheating.
10. When the display shows "Add Food" open the lid and arrange the wrapped smokies in "Crisper Basket" in a single layer.
11. Close the Ninja Foodi Grill with a lid and set the time for 10 minutes.
12. Press "Start/Stop" to begin cooking.
13. Flip the smokies once halfway through.
14. When cooking time is completed, press "Start/Stop" to stop cooking and open the lid.

Nutrition:

- Calories: 384
- Fat: 30.6 g
- Sat fat: 10.4 g
- Carbs: 7.3 g
- Fiber: 0 g
- Sugar: 6.7 g
- Protein: 19.2 g

48. Crispy Shrimp

Preparation time: 20 minutes
Cooking time: 20 minutes
Serving: 4
Ingredients:

- 1 lb. shrimp, peeled and deveined
- Salt and freshly ground black pepper, to taste
- 8 oz. coconut milk
- 1/2 cup panko breadcrumbs
- 1/2 tsp. cayenne pepper

Directions:

1. In a shallow dish, mix together the coconut milk, salt, and black pepper.
2. In another shallow dish, mix together breadcrumbs, cayenne pepper, salt, and black pepper.
3. Dip the shrimp in coconut milk mixture and then coat with the breadcrumb's mixture.
4. Arrange the "Crisper Basket" in the pot of Ninja Foodi Grill.
5. Close the Ninja Foodi Grill with lid and select "Air Crisp."
6. Set the temperature to 350°F to preheat.
7. Press "Start/Stop" to begin preheating.
8. When the display shows "Add Food" open the lid and place the shrimp into the "Crisper Basket."
9. Close the Ninja Foodi Grill with a lid and set the time for 20 minutes.
10. Press "Start/Stop" to begin cooking.
11. When cooking time is completed, press "Start/Stop" to stop cooking and open the lid.
12. Serve warm.

Nutrition:

- Calories: 301 Fat: 15.7 g
- Sat fat: 12.6 g
- Carbs: 12.5 g
- Fiber: 2.3 g
- Sugar: 2.2 g
- Protein: 28.2 g

49. Bacon-Wrapped Shrimp

Preparation time: 15 minutes
Cooking time: 7 minutes
Serving: 6
Ingredients:

- 1 lb. bacon, thinly sliced
- 1 lb. shrimp, peeled and deveined

Directions:

1. Wrap each shrimp with one bacon slice.
2. Arrange the shrimp in a baking dish and refrigerate for about 20 minutes.
3. Arrange the "Crisper Basket" in the pot of Ninja Foodi Grill.
4. Close the Ninja Foodi Grill with lid and select "Air Crisp."
5. Set the temperature to 390°F to preheat.
6. Press "Start/Stop" to begin preheating.
7. When the display shows "Add Food" open the lid and place the shrimp in the "Crisper Basket" in a single layer.
8. Close the Ninja Foodi Grill with a lid and set the time for 7 minutes.
9. Press "Start/Stop" to begin cooking.
10. When cooking time is completed, press "Start/Stop" to stop cooking and open the lid.
11. Serve warm.

Nutrition:

- Calories: 499
- Fat: 32.9 g
- Sat fat: 10.8 g
- Carbs: 2.2 g
- Fiber: 0 g
- Sugar: 0 g
- Protein: 42.5 g

50. Mozzarella Flatbread

Preparation time: 10 minutes
Cooking time: 5 minutes
Serving: 10
Ingredients:

- 1 tube prepared pizza dough
- 1/2 cup butter
- 1 tsp. garlic
- Pinch of dried parsley
- 2 cups mozzarella cheese, shredded

Directions:

1. Open and unroll the pizza dough.
2. From the long side, reroll the dough.
3. Cut 1-inch rolls from the dough and then flatten each roll.
4. In a bowl, add the butter, garlic, mozzarella cheese, and parsley and mix well.
5. Brush the top of the dough with a butter mixture.
6. Arrange the greased "Crisper Basket" in the pot of Ninja Foodi Grill.
7. Close the Ninja Foodi Grill with lid and select "Air Crisp."
8. Set the temperature to 350°F to preheat.
9. Press "Start/Stop" to begin preheating.
10. When the display shows "Add Food" open the lid and place the rolls in the "Crisper Basket" in a single layer.
11. Close the Ninja Foodi Grill with a lid and set the time for 5 minutes.
12. Press "Start/Stop" to begin cooking.
13. When cooking time is completed, press "Start/Stop" to stop cooking and open the lid.
14. Place the rolls onto a wire rack for about 5 minutes before serving.

Nutrition:

- Calories: 126
- Fat: 12.1 g
- Sat fat: 6.9 g
- Carbs: 2.8 g
- Fiber: 0.2 g
- Sugar: 0 g
- Protein: 2.1 g

51. Onion Dip

Preparation time: 10 minutes
Cooking time: 35 minutes
Serving: 8
Ingredients:

- 2/3 cup onion, chopped
- 1 cup cheddar Jack cheese, shredded
- 1/2 cup Swiss cheese, shredded
- 1/4 cup Parmesan cheese, shredded
- 2/3 cup whipped salad dressing
- 1/2 cup milk
- Salt, to taste

Directions:

1. In a large bowl, add all the ingredients and mix well.
2. Transfer the mixture into a baking pan and spread in an even layer.
3. Arrange the "Crisper Basket" in the pot of Ninja Foodi Grill.
4. Close the Ninja Foodi Grill with lid and select "Bake."
5. Set the temperature to 375°F to preheat.
6. Press "Start/Stop" to begin preheating.
7. When the display shows "Add Food" open the lid and place the pan into the "Crisper Basket."
8. Close the Ninja Foodi Grill with a lid and set the time for 45 minutes.
9. Press "Start/Stop" to begin cooking.
10. When cooking time is completed, press "Start/Stop" to stop cooking and open the lid.
11. Serve hot.

Nutrition:

- Calories: 108
- Fat: 7.5 g
- Sat fat: 4.4 g
- Carbs: 2.8 g
- Fiber: 0.3 g
- Sugar: 1.4 g
- Protein: 6.4 g

52. Spinach Dip

Preparation time: 15 minutes
Cooking time: 35 minutes
Serving: 8
Ingredients:

- 1 (8-oz.) package cream cheese, softened
- 1 cup mayonnaise
- 1 cup Parmesan cheese, grated
- 1 cup frozen spinach, thawed and squeezed
- 1/3 cup water chestnuts, drained and chopped
- 1/2 cup onion, minced
- 1/4 tsp. garlic powder
- Freshly ground black pepper, to taste

Directions:

1. In a bowl, add all the ingredients and mix until well combined.
2. Transfer the mixture into a baking pan and spread in an even layer.
3. Arrange the "Crisper Basket" in the pot of Ninja Foodi Grill.
4. Close the Ninja Foodi Grill with lid and select "Bake."
5. Set the temperature to 300°F to preheat.
6. Press "Start/Stop" to begin preheating.
7. When the display shows "Add Food" open the lid and place the pan into the "Crisper Basket."
8. Close the Ninja Foodi Grill with a lid and set the time for 30 minutes.
9. Press "Start/Stop" to begin cooking.
10. Stir the dip once halfway through.
11. When cooking time is completed, press "Start/Stop" to stop cooking and open the lid.
12. Serve hot.

Nutrition:

- Calories: 258
- Fat: 22.1 g
- Sat fat: 8.9 g
- Carbs: 9.4 g
- Fiber: 0.3 g
- Sugar: 2.3 g
- Protein: 6.7 g

53. Honey-Glazed Grilled Carrots

Preparation time: 10 minutes
Cooking time: 10 minutes
Serving: 4
Ingredients:

- 6 medium carrots, peeled and cut lengthwise
- 1 tbsp. canola oil
- 2 tbsp. unsalted butter, melted
- 1/4 cup brown sugar, melted
- 1/4 cup honey
- 1/8 tsp. sea salt

Directions:

1. Insert the Grill Grate and close the hood. Select GRILL, set the temperature to MAX, and set the time to 10 minutes. Select START/STOP to start preheating.
2. In a large bowl, toss the carrots and oil until well coated.
3. When the unit has preheated, place the carrots in the center of the Grill Grate. Close the lid and cook for 5 minutes.
4. Meanwhile, in a small bowl, whisk together the butter, brown sugar, honey, and salt.
5. After 5 minutes, open the lid and baste the carrots with the glaze. Using tongs, turn the carrots and baste the other side. Close the hood and cook for another 5 minutes.
6. When cooking is complete, serve them immediately.

Nutrition:

- Calories: 218
- Fat: 9 g
- Sat fat: 4 g
- Cholesterol: 15 mg
- Sodium: 119 mg
- Carbs: 35 g
- Fiber: 2 g
- Protein: 1 g

54. Crispy Rosemary Potatoes

Preparation time: 10 minutes
Cooking time: 20 minutes
Serving: 4
Ingredients:

- 2 lb. baby red potatoes, quartered
- 2 tbsp. extra-virgin olive oil
- 1/4 cup dried onion flakes
- 1 tsp. dried rosemary
- 1/2 tsp. onion powder
- 1/2 tsp. garlic powder
- 1/4 tsp. celery
- 1/4 tsp. freshly ground black pepper
- 1/2 tsp. dried parsley
- 1/2 tsp. sea salt

Directions:

1. Insert the basket and close the hood. Select AIR FRYER, set the temperature to 390°F, and set the time to 20 minutes. Select START/STOP to start preheating.
2. Meanwhile, place all the ingredients in a large bowl and toss until evenly coated.
3. When the unit beeps to indicate it has preheated, add the potatoes to the basket. Close the lid and cook for 10 minutes.
4. After 10 minutes, check for desired crispness. Continue cooking up to 5 more minutes if necessary.

Nutrition:

- Calories: 232
- Fat: 7 g
- Sat fat: 1 g
- Cholesterol: 0 mg
- Sodium: 249 mg
- Carbs: 39 g
- Fiber: 6 g
- Protein: 4 g.

55. Mayonnaise Corn

Preparation time: 5 to 10 minutes
Cooking time: 14 minutes
Serving: 3 to 4
Ingredients:

- 1/4 cup sour cream
- 1/4 cup mayonnaise
- 3 ears corn, husked, rinsed, and dried
- Olive oil spray
- 1/2 tsp. garlic powder
- 1/4 tsp. chili powder
- 1/4 cup crumbled cotija cheese
- 1 tsp. freshly squeezed lime juice
- Fresh cilantro leaves, for garnish
- 1/2 tsp. salt
- 1/2 tsp. Black pepper (ground)

Directions:

1. Take the Ninja Foodi Grill, arrange it over a cooking platform, and open the top lid.
2. In the unit, place the basket and coat it with some cooking spray. In the basket, add the corn and close the lid.
3. Select the "AIR FRYER" mode and adjust the 400°F temperature level. Then, set the timer to 12 minutes and press "STOP/START," which will start the cooking process. Shake the basket after 6 minutes.
4. When the timer goes off, open the lid. Add the corn to a plate.
5. In a mixing bowl, stir together the sour cream, mayonnaise, cheese, lime juice, garlic powder, and chili powder.
6. Add the cream mixture over the corn. Season to taste with salt and black pepper. Top with cilantro and more chili powder.

Nutrition:

- Calories: 265
- Fat: 13.5 g Sat fat: 5 g
- Trans fat: 0 g Carbs: 29 g
- Fiber: 4 g Sodium: 687 mg
- Protein: 7.5 g.

56. Basil Shrimp Appetizer

Preparation time: 5 to 10 minutes
Cooking time: 8 minutes
Serving: 4 to 6
Ingredients:

- 2 tsp. olive oil
- Black pepper (ground) and salt to taste
- 1 lb. shrimp, peeled and deveined
- 1 tbsp. basil, chopped

Directions:

1. Take a Ninja Foodi Grill, arrange it over a cooking platform, and open the top lid.
2. In the unit, place the basket. Add all the ingredients and combine them.
3. Select the "Air Fryer" mode and adjust the 370°F temperature level. Then, set the timer to 8 minutes and press "STOP/START," which will start the cooking process.
4. When the timer goes off, open the lid. Serve it warm.

Nutrition:

- Calories: 117
- Fat: 5 g
- Sat fat: 1 g
- Trans fat: 0 g
- Carbs: 2 g
- Fiber: 0 g
- Sodium: 924 mg
- Protein: 15 g.

57. Baked Banana

Preparation time: 10 minutes
Cooking time: 10 minutes
Serving: 4
Ingredients:

- 2 tbsp. dry shredded coconuts
- 1/4 tsp. ground cinnamon
- 2 medium (7" to 7 to 7/8" long) bananas to be cut into bite-size pieces
- 1/3 cup dry breadcrumbs
- 1 tsp. white sugar
- 1 egg white

Directions:

1. Preheat the Ninja Foodi Grill to 350°F (175°C). Line the baking sheet with parchment paper.
2. Combine coconut, breadcrumbs, cinnamon, and sugar in a bowl. Beat egg white in a small bowl until it becomes frothy. Dip each banana piece in egg white and press into the bread crumb mixture. Then put the breaded bananas on the already prepared baking sheet.
3. Bake until it turns golden brown in about 10 minutes.

Nutrition:

- Calories: 111.8
- Carbs: 20.8 g
- Protein: 3 g
- Fat: 2.6 g
- Sodium: 81.4 mg.

58. Air Fryer Avocado Fries

Preparation time: 10 minutes
Cooking time: 5 minutes
Serving: 2
Ingredients:

- 1/4 cup all-purpose flour
- 1/4 tsp. salt
- 1 tsp. water
- 1/2 cup panko breadcrumbs
- 1/2 tsp. ground black pepper
- 1 egg
- 1 ripe avocado, should be halved, seeded, and peeled before cutting into 8 slices
- 1 serving cooking spray

Directions:

1. Select Air Fryer and Preheat the Ninja Foodi Grill to about 400°F (200°C).
2. Mix the pepper, flour, and salt in a shallow bowl. Get another shallow bowl and beat water and egg together in it. Then put panko in a third shallow bowl.
3. Dredge an avocado slice through the flour, but you should shake off any excess. Dip into the egg and let the excess fall off. Finally, press the slice into the panko so that both sides are well covered. Set it on a plate and repeat this process with the remaining slices.
4. Spray avocado slices generously with cooking spray and arrange them in the Ninja Foodi basket, they should be sprayed side-down. Spray the top part of the avocado slices also.
5. Cook in the already preheated Ninja Foodi for about 4 minutes. Turn the avocado slices over and cook until they become golden in about 3 minutes.

Nutrition:

- Calories: 319 Carbs: 39.8 g
- Protein: 9.3 g
- Fat: 18 g
- Cholesterol: 81.8 mg
- Sodium: 452.9 mg.

59. Mexican Street Corn Queso Dip

Preparation time: 10 minutes
Cooking time: 20 minutes
Serving: 8
Ingredients:

- 1 (8 oz.) package cream cheese, quartered
- 6 oz. cotija cheese, crumbled, 2 oz. reserved for topping
- 1 (10 oz.) can fire-roasted tomatoes with chiles
- 1/2 cup mayonnaise - Zest of 2 limes
- Juice of 2 limes - 2 (8 oz.) packages shredded Mexican cheese blend, divided - 1 garlic clove, grated
- 1 (14.75-oz.) can cream corn
- 1 cup frozen corn - Kosher salt to taste
- Freshly ground black pepper to taste

Directions:

1. Pour the cream cheese, 4 oz. cotija cheese, tomatoes with chiles, mayonnaise, lime zest, and juice, one 8-oz. package Mexican cheese blend, garlic, cream corn, and frozen corn in the pot of the Ninja Foodi. Season with salt and pepper and stir. Close the lid.
2. Select BAKE/ROAST. Set the temperature to 375°F and the time to 20 minutes. Select START/STOP to begin.
3. After 10 minutes, open the lid and sprinkle the dip with the remaining 2 oz. of cotija cheese and the remaining 8 oz. package of Mexican blend cheese. Close the lid and continue cooking.
4. When cooking is complete, the cheese will be melted and the dip hot and bubbling at the edges. Open the lid and let the dip cool for 5 to 10 minutes before serving. Serve topped with chopped cilantro, hot sauce, and chili powder if desired.

Nutrition:

- Calories: 538 Fat: 45 g
- Sat fat: 22 g Cholesterol: 109 mg
- Sodium: 807 mg Carbs: 18 g
- Fiber: 2 g Protein: 20 g.

60. Zucchini Chips

Preparation time: 15 minutes
Cooking time: 13 minutes
Serving: 6
Ingredients:

- 1 large egg, beaten
- 3/4 cup panko bread crumbs
- 1 tsp. Old Bay seasoning
- 1 tsp. garlic salt
- 1/2 tsp. kosher salt
- 2 large zucchinis, ends trimmed cut into 1/4- to 1/2-inch rounds (the thinner the crispier)
- Olive oil spray

Directions:

1. Place the basket into the unit. Select AIR FRYER; set the temperature to 350°F and the time to 4 minutes to preheat. Select START/STOP to begin.
2. Place the beaten egg in a shallow bowl. In another shallow bowl, stir together the panko, Old Bay seasoning, garlic salt, and kosher salt.
3. One at a time, dip the zucchini rounds into the egg and the panko mixture, coating all sides. Working in batches as needed, place the coated zucchini chips in the basket in a single layer so they do not overlap. Coat the pieces with cooking spray and place them into the preheated Basket.
4. Set the time to 13 minutes and start. After 10 minutes, flip the zucchini. Close the lid and cook for 3 more minutes, or longer for crispier results.
5. Remove and repeat with the second batch.

Nutrition:

- Calories: 59
- Fat: 2 g
- Sat fat: 0 g
- Cholesterol: 31 mg
- Sodium: 374 mg
- Carbs: 9 g
- Fiber: 2 g
- Protein: 3 g

CHAPTER 5:

Poultry

61. Grilled BBQ Turkey

Preparation time: 5 to 10 minutes
Cooking time: 30 minutes
Serving: 5 to 6
Ingredients:

- 1/2 cup minced parsley
- 1/2 cup chopped green onions
- 4 garlic cloves, minced
- 1 cup Greek yogurt
- 1/2 cup lemon juice
- 1 tsp. dried rosemary, crushed
- 1/3 cup canola oil
- 4 tbsp. minced dill
- 1 tsp. salt
- 1/2 tsp. pepper
- 1-3 lb. turkey breast half, bone-in

Directions:

1. In a mixing bowl, combine all the ingredients except the turkey. Add and coat the turkey evenly. Refrigerate for 8 hours to marinate.
2. Take Ninja Foodi Grill, arrange it over your kitchen platform, and open the top lid.
3. Arrange the Grill Grate and close the top lid.
4. Press "grill" and select the "high" grill function. Adjust the timer to 30 minutes and then press "start/stop." Ninja Foodi will start pre-heating.
5. Ninja Foodi is preheated and ready to cook when it starts to beep. After you hear a beep, open the top lid.
6. Arrange the turkey over the grill grate.
7. Close the top lid and cook for 15 minutes. Now open the top lid, flip the turkey.
8. Close the top lid and cook for 15 more minutes. Cook until the food thermometer reaches 165°F.
9. Slice and serve.

Nutrition:

- Calories: 426 Fat: 8.5 g
- Carbs: 22 g Fiber: 3 g
- Sodium: 594 mg Protein: 38 g

62. Sweet and Sour Chicken BBQ

Preparation time: 10 minutes
Cooking time: 40 minutes
Serving: 4
Ingredients:

- 6 chicken drumsticks
- 3/4 cup of sugar
- 1 cup of soy sauce
- 1 cup of water
- 1/4 cup garlic, minced
- 1/4 cup tomato paste
- 3/4 cup onion, minced
- 1 cup white vinegar
- Salt and pepper, to taste

Directions:

1. Take a Ziploc bag and add all ingredients to it.
2. Marinate for at least 2 hours in your refrigerator.
3. Insert the crisper basket, and close the hood.
4. Pre-heat Ninja Foodi by squeezing the "AIR CRISP" alternative at 390°F for 40 minutes.
5. Place the grill pan accessory in the Grill.
6. Flip the chicken after every 10 minutes.
7. Take a saucepan and pour the marinade into it and heat over medium flame until sauce thickens.
8. Brush with the glaze.

Nutrition:

- Calories: 460
- Fat: 20 g
- Carbs: 26 g
- Fiber: 3 g
- Sodium: 126 mg
- Protein: 28 g

63. The Tarragon Chicken Meal

Preparation time: 10 minutes
Cooking time: 5 minutes
Serving: 4
Ingredients:
For chicken:

- 1 1/2 lb. chicken tenders
- Salt as needed
- 3 tbsp. tarragon leaves, chopped
- 1 tsp. lemon zest, grated
- 2 tbsp. fresh lemon juice
- 2 tbsp. extra virgin olive oil
- Pepper to taste

For sauce:

- 2 tbsp. fresh lemon juice   - 2 tbsp. butter, salted
- 1/2 cup heavy whip cream

Directions:

1. Prepare your chicken by taking a baking dish and arranging the chicken over the dish in a single layer. Season generously with salt and pepper.
2. Sprinkle chopped tarragon and lemon zest all around the tenders.
3. Drizzle lemon juice and olive oil on top.
4. Let them sit for 10 minutes.
5. Drain them well.
6. Insert Grill Grate in your Ninja Foodi Grill, select GRILL mode, and set to HIGH temperature. Set timer to 4 minutes.
7. Once you hear the beep, place chicken tenders in your grill grate.
8. Let it cook for 3 to 4 minutes until cooked completely. Do in batches if needed.
9. Transfer the cooked chicken tenders to a platter.
10. For the sauce, take a small-sized saucepan.
11. Add cream, butter, and lemon juice and bring to a boil. Once thick enough, pour the mix over the chicken. Serve and enjoy!

Nutrition:

- Calories: 263 Fat: 18 g
- Carbs: 7 g Fiber: 1 g
- Sodium: 363 mg
- Protein: 19 g

64. Alfredo Chicken Apples

Preparation time: 5 to 10 minutes
Cooking time: 20 minutes
Serving: 4
Ingredients:

- 1 large apple, wedged
- 1 tbsp. lemon juice
- 4 chicken breasts, halved
- 4 tsp. chicken seasoning
- 4 slices provolone cheese
- 1/4 cup blue cheese, crumbled
- 1/2 cup Alfredo sauce

Directions:

1. Take a bowl and add chicken, season it well.
2. Take another bowl and add in apple, lemon juice.
3. Pre-heat Ninja Foodi by pressing the "GRILL" option and setting it to "MEDIUM" and timer to 20 minutes.
4. Let it pre-heat until you hear a beep.
5. Arrange chicken over Grill Grate, lock lid and cook for 8 minutes, flip and cook for 8 minutes more. Add provolone cheese, blue cheese, and Alfredo sauce.
6. Grill apple in the same manner for 2 minutes per side.

Nutrition:

- Calories: 247
- Fat: 19 g
- Carbs: 29 g
- Fiber: 6 g
- Sodium: 853 mg
- Protein: 14 g

65. Hearty Chicken Zucchini Kabobs

Preparation time: 10 minutes
Cooking time: 15 minutes
Serving: 4
Ingredients:

- 1 lb. chicken breast, boneless, skinless, and cut into cubes of 2 inches
- 2 tbsp. Greek yogurt, plain
- 4 lemons juice
- 1 lemon zest
- 1/4 cup extra-virgin olive oil
- 2 tbsp. oregano
- 1 red onion, quartered
- 1 zucchini, sliced
- 4 garlic cloves, minced
- 1 tsp. sea salt
- 1/2 tsp. ground black pepper

Directions:

1. Take a mixing bowl, add olive oil, Greek yogurt, lemon juice, oregano, garlic, zest, salt, and pepper, combine them well.
2. Add the chicken and coat well, refrigerate for 1 to 2 hours to marinate.
3. Arrange the grill grate and close the lid.
4. Pre-heat Ninja Foodi by pressing the "GRILL" option and setting it to "MEDIUM" and timer to 7 minutes.
5. Take the skewers, thread the chicken, zucchini and red onion and thread alternatively.
6. Let it pre-heat until you hear a beep.
7. Arrange the skewers over the grill grate lock lid and cook until the timer reads zero.
8. Baste the kebabs with a marinating mixture in between.
9. Take out your dish when it reaches 165°F.
10. Serve warm and enjoy.

Nutrition:

- Calories: 277 Fat: 15 g
- Carbs: 10 g Fiber: 2 g Sodium: 146 mg

66. Delicious Maple Glazed Chicken

Preparation time: 10 minutes
Cooking time: 15 minutes
Serving: 4
Ingredients:

- 2 lb. chicken wings, bone-in
- 1 tsp. black pepper, ground
- 1/4 cup teriyaki sauce
- 1 cup maple syrup
- 1/3 cup soy sauce
- 3 garlic cloves, minced
- 2 tsp. garlic powder
- 2 tsp. onion powder

Directions:

1. Take a mixing bowl, add garlic, soy sauce, black pepper, maple syrup, garlic powder, onion powder, and teriyaki sauce, combine well.
2. Add the chicken wings and combine well to coat.
3. Arrange the Grill Grate and close the lid.
4. Pre-heat Ninja Foodi by pressing the "GRILL" option and setting it to "MEDIUM" and timer to 10 minutes.
5. Let it pre-heat until you hear a beep.
6. Arrange the chicken wings over the grill grate lock lid and cook for 5 minutes.
7. Flip the chicken and close the lid, cook for 5 minutes more.
8. Serve warm and enjoy!

Nutrition:

- Calories: 543
- Fat: 26 g
- Carbs: 46 g
- Fiber: 4 g
- Sodium: 648 mg
- Protein: 42 g

67. Grilled Orange Chicken

Preparation time: 5 to 10 minutes
Cooking time: 10 minutes
Serving: 5 to 6
Ingredients:

- 2 tsp. ground coriander
- 1/2 tsp. garlic salt
- 1/4 tsp. ground black pepper
- 12 chicken wings
- 1 tbsp. canola oil

Sauce:

- 1/4 cup butter, melted
- 3 tbsp. honey
- 1/2 cup orange juice
- 1/3 cup Sriracha chili sauce
- 2 tbsp. lime juice
- 1/4 cup chopped cilantro

Directions:

1. Coat chicken with oil and season with the spices; refrigerate for 2 hours to marinate.
2. Combine all the sauce ingredients and set them aside. Optionally, you can stir-cook the sauce mixture for 3 to 4 minutes in a saucepan.
3. Take Ninja Foodi Grill, organize it over your kitchen stage, and open the top cover.
4. Organize the barbecue mesh and close the top cover. Click "grill" and choose the "med" grill function. Adjust the timer to 10 minutes and afterward press "start/stop." Ninja Foodi will begin pre-warming. Ninja Foodi is preheated and prepared to cook when it begins to signal. After you hear a blare, open the top.
5. Organize chicken over the grill grate.
6. Close the top lid and cook for 5 minutes. Now open the top lid, flip the chicken.
7. Close the top lid and cook for 5 more minutes.

Nutrition:

- Calories: 327 Fat: 14 g
- Carbs: 19 g Fiber: 1 g Sodium: 258 mg
- Protein: 25 g

68. Baked Coconut Chicken

Preparation time: 10 minutes
Cooking time: 12 minutes
Serving: 4
Ingredients:

- 2 large eggs
- 2 tsp. garlic powder
- 1 tsp. salt
- 1/2 tsp. ground black pepper
- 3/4 cup almond meal
- 3/4 cup coconut aminos
- 1 lb. chicken tenders
- Cooking spray as needed

Directions:

1. Pre-heat Ninja Foodi by squeezing the "air crisp" alternative and setting it to "400°F" and timer to 12 minutes.
2. Take a large-sized baking sheet and spray it with cooking spray.
3. Take a wide dish and add garlic powder, eggs, pepper, and salt.
4. Whisk well until everything is combined.
5. Add the almond meal and coconut and mix well.
6. Take your chicken tenders and dip them in the egg followed by dipping in the coconut mix.
7. Shake off any excess.
8. Transfer them to your Ninja Foodi Grill and spray the tenders with a bit of oil.
9. Cook for 12 to 14 minutes until you have a nice golden-brown texture.

Nutrition:

- Calories: 180
- Fat: 1 g
- Carbs: 3 g
- Fiber: 1 g
- Sodium: 214 mg
- Protein: 0 g

69. Spinach Turkey Burgers

Preparation time: 15 minutes
Cooking time: 19 minutes
Serving: 8
Ingredients:

- 1 tbsp. avocado oil
- 2 lbs. turkey ground
- 2 shallots, chopped
- 2 1/2 cups spinach, chopped
- 3 garlic cloves, minced
- 2/3 cup feta cheese, crumbled
- 3/4 tsp. Greek seasoning
- 1/2 tsp. salt
- 1/4 tsp. black pepper
- 8 hamburger buns, split

Directions:

1. Start by sautéing shallots in a skillet for 2 minutes, then add garlic and spinach.
2. Cook for 45 seconds, then transfer to a suitable bowl.
3. Add all the seasoning, beef, and feta cheese to the bowl.
4. Mix well, then make 8 patties of 1/2 inch thickness.
5. Preheat the Ninja Foodi Grill on the "Grill Mode" at MEDIUM-temperature settings.
6. When the grill is preheated, open its hood and place the 2 patties in it.
7. Cover the grill's hood and grill for 8 minutes.
8. Flip the patties and continue grilling for another 8 minutes.
9. Grill the remaining patties in a similar way.
10. Serve the patties in between the buns with desired toppings.
11. Enjoy.

Nutrition:

- Calories: 529 Fat: 17 g
- Sodium: 422 mg Carbs: 55 g
- Fiber: 0 g
- Sugar: 1 g
- Protein: 41 g

70. Barbecued Turkey

Preparation time: 15 minutes
Cooking time: 30 minutes
Serving: 6
Ingredients:

- 1 cup Greek yogurt
- 1/2 cup lemon juice
- 1/3 cup canola oil
- 1/2 cup fresh parsley, minced
- 1 (3 lbs.) turkey breast half, bone-in
- 1/2 cup green onions, chopped
- 4 garlic cloves, minced
- 4 tbsp. dill, fresh minced
- 1 tsp. dried rosemary, crushed
- 1 tsp. salt
- 1/2 tsp. black pepper

Directions:

1. Take the first 10 ingredients in a bowl and mix well.
2. Mix turkey with this marinade in a suitable bowl for seasoning.
3. Cover it to marinate for 8 hours of marination.
4. Preheat the Ninja Foodi Grill on the "Grill Mode" at MEDIUM-temperature settings.
5. When the grill is preheated, open its hood and place the turkey in it.
6. Cover the grill's hood and grill for 15 minutes.
7. Flip the turkey and continue grilling for another 15 minutes until al dente.
8. Grill until the internal temperature reaches 165°F.
9. Slice and serve.

Nutrition:

- Calories: 440
- Fat: 14 g
- Sodium: 220 mg
- Carbs: 22 g
- Fiber: 0.2 g
- Sugar: 1 g
- Protein: 37 g

71. Grilled Chicken Wings With Jaew

Preparation time: 15 minutes
Cooking time: 30 minutes
Serving: 4
Ingredients:
Jaew:

- 1/2 cup fish sauce
- 3 tbsp. fresh lime juice
- 2 tbsp. granulated sugar
- 2 tsp. red Thai chile powder
- 1 1/2 tsp. toasted sesame seeds

Wings:
- 1/3 cup oyster sauce
- 1/4 cup Thai seasoning sauce
- 2 tbsp. granulated sugar - 2 tbsp. vegetable oil
- 1 1/2 tsp. black pepper
- 30 chicken wing flats

Directions:
1. Place the cooking pot in the Ninja Foodi Grill then set a grill grate inside.
2. Mix chile powder, sugar, lime juice, and fish sauce in a bowl.
3. Stir in sesame seeds, and mix well then keep 3 tbsp. marinade aside.
4. Mix the remaining marinade with the chicken in a large bowl. Cover and refrigerate for 30 minutes for marination. Mix the reserved marinade and remaining ingredients in a bowl.
5. Thread the chicken on the wooden skewers and brush the prepared glaze over them.
6. Select the "Grill" Mode, set the temperature to MED. Press the START/STOP button to initiate preheating. Once preheated, place the chicken in the Ninja Foodi Grill.
7. Cover the hood and cook for 10 to 15 minutes per side until golden brown and tender.
8. Serve warm.

Nutrition:
- Calories: 344 Fat: 13 g
- Sodium: 216 mg Carbs: 7 g
- Fiber: 3 g Sugar: 4 g Protein: 31 g

72. Grilled Chicken With Banana Pepper Dip

Preparation time: 15 minutes
Cooking time: 28 minutes
Serving: 6
Ingredients:

- 3 tbsp. olive oil
- 2 medium banana peppers sliced
- 4 oz. feta cheese, crumbled
- 3 tsp. fresh lemon juice
- 1/2 tsp. kosher salt
- 1/4 tsp. black pepper
- 1 oz. pita bread
- 1 (6-oz.) boneless chicken breast
- 4 grape tomatoes, halved
- 1 small Persian cucumber, halved
- 1 tbsp. red onion, chopped
- 5 pitted kalamata olives, halved
- 2 tsp. torn fresh mint

Directions:
1. Sauté banana peppers with 1 tbsp. oil in a skillet for 6 minutes.
2. Allow them to cool then blend with 2 tbsp. lemon juice in a blender until smooth.
3. Stir in black pepper and salt then mix well.
4. Rub the chicken with black pepper, salt, and oil.
5. Place the cooking pot in the Ninja Foodi Grill then set a grill grate inside.
6. Select the "Grill" Mode, set the temperature to MED. Press the START/STOP button to initiate preheating. Once preheated, place the chicken in the Ninja Foodi Grill. Cover the hood and allow the grill to cook for 7 minutes per side.
7. Transfer the chicken to a plate and cook the pita for 4 minutes per side.
8. Mix tomatoes with other ingredients in a bowl.
9. Slice the chicken and serve with banana pepper dip, pita, and tomato mixture. Serve.

Nutrition:
- Calories: 348 Fat: 12 g Sodium: 710 mg
- Carbs: 24 g Fiber: 5 g Sugar: 3 g
- Protein: 34 g

73. Huli Huli Chicken Wings

Preparation time: 15 minutes
Cooking time: 33 minutes
Serving: 6
Ingredients:

- 1 cup unsweetened pineapple juice
- 1 cup chicken stock - 1/2 cup soy sauce
- 1/2 cup packed light brown sugar
- 1/3 cup ketchup
- 2 tsp. grated peeled fresh ginger
- 1 1/2 tsp. garlic, chopped
- 2 lbs. whole chicken wings - 1/2 tsp. kosher salt
- 1 (3 lb.) fresh pineapple, peeled and cut into 1/2 -inch slices
- Sliced scallions to taste

Directions:

1. Mix pineapple juice, garlic, ginger, ketchup, brown sugar, soy sauce, and stock in a bowl
2. Keep 1 cup of this marinade aside and mix the remaining chicken in a Ziplock bag.
3. Seal the bag, and refrigerate for 3 hours for marination. Remove the chicken from the marinade and season with salt.
4. Place the cooking pot in the Ninja Foodi Grill then set a grill grate inside.
5. Select the "Grill" Mode, set the temperature to MED. Press the START/STOP button to initiate preheating.
6. Once preheated, place the chicken in the Ninja Foodi Grill. Cover the hood and allow the grill to cook for 15 minutes. Flip the chicken pieces and grill for another 10 minutes.
7. Grill the pineapple pieces for 4 minutes per side.
8. Pour the remaining marinade over the chicken and garnish it with scallions.
9. Serve warm with grilled pineapple.

Nutrition:

- Calories: 373 Fat: 8 g
- Sodium: 146 mg Carbs: 28 g
- Fiber: 5 g Sugar: 1 g Protein: 23 g

74. Kewpie-Marinated Chicken

Preparation time: 15 minutes
Cooking time: 25 minutes
Serving: 6
Ingredients:

- 1 cup Kewpie mayonnaise
- 2 tsp. lime zest
- 1 1/2 tbsp. ground cumin
- 1 1/2 tbsp. hot paprika
- 1 tbsp. kosher salt
- 1 tsp. black pepper
- 2 (3-lb.) whole chickens, cut into pieces
- Olive oil, for brushing

Directions:

1. Mix mayonnaise with 1 tsp. black pepper, 1 tbsp. salt, paprika, cumin, and lime juice, and zest.
2. Remove the chicken bones and flatten the meat with a mallet.
3. Cut slits over the chicken and place them in a tray.
4. Spread and rub the prepared marinade over the chicken.
5. Cover and refrigerate for 2 hours.
6. Place the cooking pot in the Ninja Foodi Grill then set a grill grate inside.
7. Select the "Grill" Mode, set the temperature to MED.
8. Press the START/STOP button to initiate preheating.
9. Once preheated, place the chicken in the Ninja Foodi Grill.
10. Cover the hood and allow the grill to cook for 15 minutes. Flip the chicken pieces and grill again for 10 minutes.
11. Serve warm.

Nutrition:

- Calories: 375 Fat: 16 g Sodium: 255 mg
- Carbs: 4.1 g Fiber: 1.2 g
- Sugar: 5 g
- Protein: 24.1 g

75. Grilled Chicken Thighs With Pickled Peaches

Preparation time: 15 minutes
Cooking time: 22 minutes
Serving: 4
Ingredients:
Peaches:

- 6 medium peaches - 1 1/2 cups distilled white vinegar - 1 cup sugar
- 1 stalk of lemongrass, sliced
- 1 (1-inch piece) ginger, peeled and sliced
- 1/2 tsp. whole black peppercorns
- 5 allspice berries - 2 whole cloves
- 1 (3-inch) cinnamon stick

Chicken:

- 8 cups water - 1 tbsp. sorghum syrup
- Kosher salt, to taste
- Black pepper, to taste
- 8 bone-in chicken thighs
- 1/2 cup 1 tbsp. olive oil
- 1 tbsp. red wine vinegar
- 2 garlic cloves, chopped
- 1/4 cup parsley, basil, and tarragon chopped
- 4 cups arugula, thick stems discarded

Directions:

1. Mix 8 cups water with 2 tbsp. salt and sorghum syrup in a bowl Add chicken to the sorghum water and cover to refrigerate overnight.
2. Remove the chicken to a bowl, then add garlic, herbs, 1 tsp. pepper, vinegar, and 1/2 cup olive oil. Preheat the Ninja Foodi Grill on the "Grill Mode" at MEDIUM-temperature settings.
3. When the grill is preheated, open its hood and place the chicken in it.
4. Cover the grill's hood and grill for 6 minutes per side. Transfer the grilled chicken to a plate.
5. Add water to a saucepan and boil it.
6. Carve an X on top of the peaches and boil them in the water, then cook for 2 minutes.
7. Transfer the peaches to an ice bath, then peel the peaches. Cut the peaches in half and remove the

pit from the center. Mix the rest of the ingredients for peaches and 1 1/2 cups water in a saucepan. Allow the glaze to cool, and toss in peaches. Cover and refrigerate the peaches overnight. Grill the peaches in the Ninja Foodi grill for 5 minutes per side. Serve the chicken and peaches with arugula. Enjoy.

Nutrition:

- Calories: 545 Fat: 7.9 g
- Sodium: 581 mg Carbs: 41 g
- Fiber: 2.6 g Sugar: 0.1 g Protein: 42.5 g

76. Chicken Kebabs With Currants

Preparation time: 15 minutes
Cooking time: 16 minutes
Serving: 6
Ingredients:

- 2 medium red bell peppers, cubed
- 1 cup dried currants
- 1 (14-oz.) jar sweet pickled red peppers, cubed
- 1/2 cup of the juices from pickles
- 2 tbsp. olive oil - Kosher salt, to taste
- 3 lb. boneless chicken thighs, cut into 1-inch-wide strips
- 3 lb. boneless chicken breasts, cut into strips

Directions:

1. Toss chicken with olive oil, peppers, pickle juices, salt, and currants.
2. Cover and refrigerate the chicken for 30 minutes for marination.
3. Thread the marinated chicken on the wooden skewers. Preheat the Ninja Foodi Grill on the "Grill Mode" at MEDIUM-temperature settings.
4. When the grill is preheated, open its hood and place the skewers in it.
5. Cover the grill's hood and grill for 8 minutes per side. Serve warm.

Nutrition:

- Calories: 361 Fat: 16 g Sodium: 189 mg
- Carbs: 19.3 g Fiber: 0.3 g Sugar: 18.2 g
- Protein: 33.3 g

77. Piri Piri Chicken

Preparation time: 15 minutes
Cooking time: 8 minutes
Serving: 2
Ingredients:

- 1 small red bell pepper, chopped
- 1/2 cup cilantro leaves
- 1 small shallot, chopped
- 2 tbsp. red wine vinegar
- 2 tbsp. olive oil
- 1 tbsp. paprika
- 2 garlic cloves, crushed
- 2 Piri Piri chiles stemmed
- 1 1/2 tsp. dried oregano
- 1 tbsp. kosher salt
- 1 1/4 lb. chicken pieces
- Canola oil for brushing
- 1 lb. Shishito peppers

Directions:

1. Mix the chicken piece with the rest of the ingredients in a bowl.
2. Cover and refrigerate the chicken for 30 minutes for marination.
3. Preheat the Ninja Foodi Grill on the "Grill Mode" at MEDIUM-temperature settings.
4. When the grill is preheated, open its hood and place the chicken in it.
5. Cover the grill's hood and grill for 4 minutes per side.
6. Serve warm.

Nutrition:

- Calories: 334
- Fat: 16 g
- Sodium: 462 mg
- Carbs: 31 g
- Fiber: 0.4 g
- Sugar: 3 g
- Protein: 35.3 g

78. Grilled Chicken With Grapes

Preparation time: 15 minutes
Cooking time: 35 minutes
Serving: 6
Ingredients:

- 1 cup whole buttermilk
- 1 cup water
- 1/2 cup yellow onion, sliced
- 2 tbsp. light brown sugar
- 1 1/2 tbsp. hot sauce
- 1 tbsp. salt
- 1 tsp. black pepper
- 3 garlic cloves, smashed
- 3 boneless, skin-on chicken breasts
- 6 boneless, skin-on chicken thighs
- 1 lb. Bronx grapes, separated into small clusters

Directions:

1. Mix chicken with the rest of the ingredients except the grapes.
2. Cover and marinate the chicken for 30 minutes in the refrigerator.
3. Preheat the Ninja Foodi Grill on the "Grill Mode" at MEDIUM-temperature settings.
4. When the grill is preheated, open its hood and place the chicken in it.
5. Cover the grill's hood and grill for 25 minutes.
6. Flip the chicken once cooked halfway through.
7. Grill the grapes for 5 minutes per side until slightly charred.
8. Serve chicken with grilled grapes.
9. Enjoy.

Nutrition:

- Calories: 419
- Fat: 13 g
- Sodium: 432 mg
- Carbs: 9.1 g
- Fiber: 3 g
- Sugar: 1 g
- Protein: 33 g

79. Grilled Chicken With Mustard Barbecue Sauce

Preparation time: 15 minutes
Cooking time: 20 minutes
Serving: 4
Ingredients:

- 2 tbsp. olive oil
- 1/4 cup apple cider vinegar
- 1/4 cup light brown sugar
- 2 tbsp. honey - 2 tsp. Worcestershire sauce
- 1 tsp. garlic powder - 1 tsp. paprika
- 1/4 tsp. cayenne pepper
- 1/2 cup 2 tbsp. mustard
- 6 lb. bone-in chicken breasts
- Kosher salt to taste
- 2 large sweet onions, sliced
- 1 (15 oz.) jar pickled green beans
- 2 lb. tomatoes, sliced into rounds

Directions:

1. Mix the oil, vinegar, sugar, honey, Worcestershire sauce, garlic powder, paprika, cayenne, and 1/2 cup mustard in a bowl.
2. Rub the chicken with 2 tbsp. salt.
3. Place the cooking pot in the Ninja Foodi Grill then set a grill grate inside.
4. Select the "Grill" Mode, set the temperature to MED.
5. Press the START/STOP button to initiate preheating.
6. Once preheated, place the chicken in the Ninja Foodi Grill.
7. Cover the hood and cook for 10 minutes per side. Meanwhile, mix the rest of the tomato salad ingredients (mustard, onions, green beans, and tomatoes) in a bowl. Serve the grilled chicken with this salad. Enjoy.

Nutrition:

- Calories: 401 Fat: 7 g
- Sodium: 269 mg Carbs: 25 g
- Fiber: 4 g Sugar: 12 g Protein: 26 g

80. Peruvian Chicken Skewers

Preparation time: 15 minutes
Cooking time: 10 minutes
Serving: 4
Ingredients:

- 1/2 cup ají panca paste
- 5 tbsp. olive oil
- 3 tbsp. red wine vinegar
- 2 tbsp. gochujang
- 1 tbsp. tamari or soy sauce
- 1 1/2 tsp. toasted cumin seeds
- 1/4 tsp. dried Mexican oregano
- 1/8 tsp. black pepper
- 1 large garlic clove
- 1 1/2 lbs. boneless chicken thighs, cut into cubes
- Huacatay dipping sauce to taste

Directions:

1. Mix chicken cubes with gochujang and other ingredients in a bowl.
2. Cover and refrigerate for 30 minutes then thread the chicken on the wooden skewers.
3. Place the cooking pot in the Ninja Foodi Grill then set a grill grate inside.
4. Select the "Grill" Mode, set the temperature to MED.
5. Press the START/STOP button to initiate preheating.
6. Once preheated, place the chicken in the Ninja Foodi Smart XL Grill.
7. Cover the hood and allow the grill to cook for 10 minutes, flipping halfway through.
8. Serve warm with dipping sauce.

Nutrition:

- Calories: 329 Fat: 5 g
- Sodium: 510 mg
- Carbs: 17 g
- Fiber: 5 g
- Sugar: 4 g
- Protein: 21 g

81. Grilled Wild Duck Breast

Preparation time: 15 minutes
Cooking time: 10 minutes
Serving: 8
Ingredients:

- 1/4 cup Worcestershire sauce
- 2 tbsp. olive oil
- 1/2 tsp. hot sauce
- 2 tbsp. garlic, minced
- 1/4 tsp. black pepper
- 8 boned duck breast halves

Directions:

1. Place duck breasts in a tray.
2. Mix oil and the rest of the ingredients together and then pour over the duck.
3. Rub well and cover to refrigerate for 30 minutes.
4. Place the cooking pot in the Ninja Foodi Grill then set a grill grate inside.
5. Select the "Grill" Mode, set the temperature to MED.
6. Press the START/STOP button to initiate preheating.
7. Once preheated, place the chicken in the Ninja Foodi Grill.
8. Cover the hood and cook for 5 minutes per side.
9. Serve warm.

Nutrition:

- Calories: 297
- Fat: 25 g
- Sodium: 122 mg
- Carbs: 23 g
- Fiber: 0.4 g
- Sugar: 1 g
- Protein: 43 g

82. Spice-Rubbed Duck Breast

Preparation time: 15 minutes
Cooking time: 24 minutes
Serving: 4
Ingredients:

- 2 cups orange juice
- 1-pint blackberries
- 1 tbsp. dry mustard
- 1 tbsp. sweet paprika
- 1 tsp. ground chile de Arbol
- 1/2 tsp. ground cinnamon
- 1/2 tsp. five-spice powder
- 1/2 tsp. ground coriander
- 4 duck breasts
- Kosher salt to taste
- Freshly ground black pepper to taste
- 1/2 tsp. olive oil

Directions:

1. Boil orange juice and blackberries in a saucepan and cook for 10 minutes stirring it occasionally.
2. Stir in the rest of the spices to this sauce, mix well and allow it to cool.
3. Place duck breasts in a tray then pour the sauce over the duck breasts.
4. Rub well and cover and refrigerate for 30 minutes.
5. Place the cooking pot in the Ninja Foodi Grill then set a grill grate inside.
6. Select the "Grill" Mode, set the temperature to MED.
7. Press the START/STOP button to initiate preheating.
8. Once preheated, place the chicken in the Ninja Foodi Grill.
9. Cover the hood and cook for 7 minutes per side.
10. Serve warm.

Nutrition:

- Calories: 440 Fat: 5 g
- Sodium: 244 mg Carbs: 16 g
- Fiber: 1 g Sugar: 1 g
- Protein: 27 g

83. Chicken Breasts With Pineapple Relish

Preparation time: 15 minutes
Cooking time: 15 minutes
Serving: 4
Ingredients:
Marinade:

- 1 ripe pineapple, peeled but left whole
- 1 jalapeño chile - 1/2 red onion
- 1/2 cup vinegar
- 1 tbsp. roasted garlic
- 1 tbsp. salt
- 4 boneless chicken breasts

Grilled pineapple relish:

- 1/2 peeled pineapple, chopped
- Oil, for coating - Honey, for coating
- Salt to taste
- 1 jalapeño chile
- 1/2 red onion, peeled and halved
- 1/4 cup vinegar
- 1/2 cup cilantro leaves, chopped

Directions:

1. Blend all the marinade ingredients in a blender and pour over the chicken in a bowl.
2. Mix well, cover, and refrigerate for 1 hour.
3. Meanwhile, mix the remaining relish ingredients in a bowl and keep them aside.
4. Place the cooking pot in the Ninja Foodi Grill then set a grill grate inside.
5. Select the "Grill" Mode, set the temperature to MED. Press the START/STOP button to initiate preheating. Once preheated, place the chicken in the Ninja Foodi Grill.
6. Cover the hood and cook for 10 minutes. Flip the chicken and grill again for 5 minutes.
7. Serve the chicken with relish.

Nutrition:

- Calories: 418 Fat: 22 g
- Sodium: 350 mg Carbs: 22 g
- Fiber: 0.7 g Sugar: 1 g Protein: 24.3 g

84. Chicken Thigh Yakitori

Preparation time: 15 minutes
Cooking time: 10 minutes
Serving: 4
Ingredients:

- 1/3 cup mild tare sauce
- 3 tbsp. tamari
- 1 1/2 tbsp. wasabi paste
- 4 skinless, boneless chicken thighs
- 3 scallions, cut into 1-inch lengths
- Olive oil to taste
- Salt, to taste

Directions:

1. Mix wasabi with tamari and tare sauce in a bowl.
2. Toss in chicken pieces and mix well to coat.
3. Thread these chicken pieces and scallions over the wooden skewers then drizzle oil and salt.
4. Place the cooking pot in the Ninja Foodi Grill then set a grill grate inside.
5. Select the "Grill" Mode, set the temperature to MED.
6. Press the START/STOP button to initiate preheating.
7. Once preheated, place the chicken in the Ninja Foodi Grill.
8. Cover the hood and allow the grill to cook for 5 minutes per side.
9. Serve warm.

Nutrition:

- Calories: 357
- Fat: 12 g
- Sodium: 48 mg
- Carbs: 16 g
- Fiber: 2 g
- Sugar: 0 g
- Protein: 24 g

85. Crispy Cajun Chicken

Preparation time: 10 minutes
Cooking time: 25 minutes
Serving: 2
Ingredients:

- 2 chicken breasts
- 1 tsp. Cajun seasoning
- 2 tbsp. mayonnaise
- 3/4 cup breadcrumbs
- 1 tsp. garlic powder
- 1 tsp. paprika
- Pepper to taste
- Salt to taste

Directions:

1. Place the cooking pot in the Ninja Foodi Grill Main Unit.
2. In a shallow dish, mix breadcrumbs, paprika, garlic powder, Cajun seasoning, pepper, and salt.
3. Brush chicken with mayo and coat with breadcrumb mixture.
4. Place coated chicken into the baking dish.
5. Press Bake mode, set the temperature to 400°F and set time to 25 minutes. Press Start.
6. Once a unit is preheated then place the baking dish in the cooking pot.
7. Cover with lid and cook for 25 minutes.

Nutrition:

- Calories: 503
- Fat: 18 g
- Sodium: 630 mg
- Carbs: 34.3 g
- Fiber: 2.4 g
- Sugar: 3.9 g
- Protein: 48.2 g

86. Grill Pesto Chicken Breast

Preparation time: 10 minutes
Cooking time: 30 minutes
Serving: 4
Ingredients:

- 4 chicken breasts, boneless and skinless
- 8 oz. Mozzarella cheese, sliced
- 1 tbsp. garlic, minced
- 2 tomatoes, sliced
- 1/2 cup pesto
- 2 tbsp. fresh basil
- Pepper to taste
- Salt to taste

Directions:

1. Place the cooking pot in the Ninja Foodi Grill Main Unit.
2. Place chicken into the baking dish and sprinkle with garlic and basil.
3. Pour pesto, salt, and pepper over chicken. Arrange tomato slices and cheese on top of the chicken.
4. Press Bake mode, set the temperature to 400°F and set time to 30 minutes. Press Start.
5. Once a unit is preheated then place the baking dish in the cooking pot.
6. Cover with lid and cook for 30 minutes.

Nutrition:

- Calories: 587
- Fat: 34 g
- Sodium: 698 mg
- Carbs: 7.1 g
- Fiber: 1.3 g
- Sugar: 3.6 g
- Protein: 62 g

87. Balsamic Chicken

Preparation time: 10 minutes
Cooking time: 25 minutes
Serving: 4
Ingredients:

- 4 chicken breasts, boneless & skinless
- 1/2 cup Balsamic vinegar
- 2 tbsp. soy sauce
- 1/4 cup olive oil
- 2 tsp. dried oregano
- 1 tsp. garlic, minced
- Pepper to taste
- Salt to taste

Directions:

1. Place the cooking pot in the Ninja Foodi Grill Main Unit.
2. Place chicken into the baking dish.
3. Mix together the remaining ingredients and pour over the chicken.
4. Press Bake mode, set the temperature to 400°F and set time to 25 minutes. Press Start.
5. Once a unit is preheated then place the baking dish in the cooking pot.
6. Cover with lid and cook for 25 minutes.

Nutrition:

- Calories: 399
- Fat: 23.5 g
- Sodium: 617 mg
- Carbs: 1.6 g
- Fiber: 0.4 g
- Sugar: 0.3 g
- Protein: 42.9 g

88. Marinated Grill Chicken Breast

Preparation time: 10 minutes
Cooking time: 10 minutes
Serving: 4
Ingredients:

- 4 chicken breasts, boneless & skinless

For the marinade:

- 1/2 cup orange juice
- 1 tsp. garlic, minced
- 3 tbsp. olive oil
- 1/2 tsp. allspice
- 3/4 tsp. ground nutmeg

Directions:

1. Place the cooking pot in the Ninja Foodi Grill Main Unit then place the grill plate in the pot.
2. Add chicken and marinade ingredients into the zip-lock bag. Seal bag and place in the refrigerator for 2 hours.
3. Press Grill mode, set the temperature to HIGH and set time to 10 minutes. Press Start.
4. Once a unit is preheated then place marinated chicken on the grill plate.
5. Cover with lid and cook for 10 minutes.

Nutrition:

- Calories: 385
- Fat: 21.6 g
- Sodium: 126 mg
- Carbs: 3.8 g
- Fiber: 0.2 g
- Sugar: 2.7 g
- Protein: 42.5 g

89. Greek Chicken

Preparation time: 10 minutes
Cooking time: 20 minutes
Serving: 4
Ingredients:

- 4 chicken breasts, boneless and halves
- 3 tbsp. olive oil
- 3 tbsp. capers, rinsed and drained
- 10 olives, pitted and halved
- 2 cups cherry tomatoes
- Pepper to taste
- Salt to taste

Directions:

1. Place the cooking pot in the Ninja Foodi Grill Main Unit.
2. In a bowl, mix tomatoes, capers, olives, and oil. Set aside.
3. Season chicken with pepper and salt.
4. Place chicken in the baking dish. Top with tomato mixture.
5. Press Bake mode, set the temperature to 400°F and set time to 20 minutes. Press Start.
6. Once a unit is preheated then place the baking dish in the cooking pot.
7. Cover with lid and cook for 20 minutes.

Nutrition:

- Calories: 156
- Fat: 12.6 g
- Sodium: 345 mg
- Carbs: 4.5 g
- Fiber: 1.7 g
- Sugar: 2.4 g
- Protein: 7.9 g

90. Chicken Cheese Patties

Preparation time: 10 minutes
Cooking time: 25 minutes
Serving: 4
Ingredients:

- 1 egg
- 1 lb. ground chicken
- 1/8 tsp. red pepper flakes
- 2 garlic cloves, minced
- 1/2 cup onion, minced
- 3/4 cup breadcrumbs
- 1 cup Cheddar cheese, shredded
- 1 cup carrot, grated
- 1 cup cauliflower, grated
- Pepper to taste
- Salt to taste

Directions:

1. Place the cooking pot in the Ninja Foodi Grill Main Unit.
2. Add all ingredients into the bowl and mix until well combined.
3. Make patties from the meat mixture and place them in the baking dish.
4. Press Bake mode, set the temperature to 400°F and set time to 25 minutes. Press Start.
5. Once a unit is preheated then place the baking dish in the cooking pot.
6. Cover with lid and cook for 25 minutes.

Nutrition:

- Calories: 451
- Fat: 20 g
- Sodium: 503 mg
- Carbs: 20.9 g
- Fiber: 2.6 g
- Sugar: 4.1 g
- Protein: 44.9 g

CHAPTER 6:

~ 62 ~

Beef, Pork, And Lamb

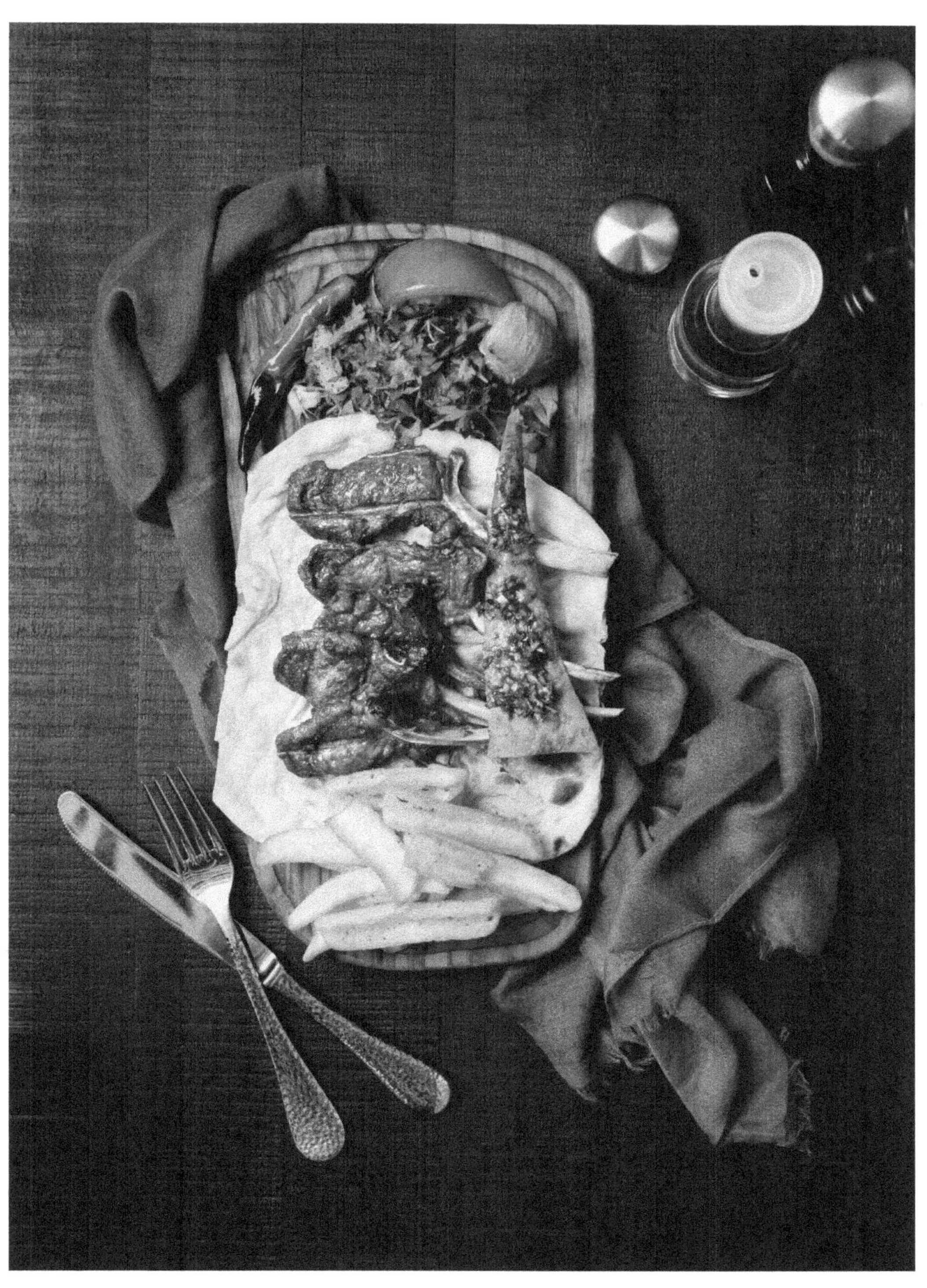

91. Honey-Glazed Pork Tenderloin

Preparation time: 5 minutes
Cooking time: 20 minutes
Serving: 4
Ingredients:

- 2 tbsp. honey
- 1 tbsp. soy sauce
- 1/2 tsp. garlic powder
- 1/2 tsp. sea salt
- 1 (1 1/2-lb.) pork tenderloin

Directions:

1. Insert the Grill Grate and close the hood. Select grill set the temperature to medium and the time to 20 minutes. Select start/stop to start preheating.
2. Meanwhile, in a small bowl, combine the honey, soy sauce, garlic powder, and salt.
3. When the unit beeps to signify it has preheated, place the pork tenderloin on the Grill Grate. Baste all sides with the honey glaze. Close the hood and cook for 8 minutes. After 8 minutes, flip the pork tenderloin and baste with any remaining glaze. Close the hood and cook for 7 more minutes.
4. Serve it and enjoy.

Nutrition:

- Calories: 215
- Fat: 6 g
- Sat fat: 2 g
- Cholesterol: 98 mg
- Sodium: 558 mg
- Carbs: 9 g
- Fiber: 0 g
- Protein: 30 g

92. Asian Style Pork Ribs

Preparation time: 5 to 10 minutes
Cooking time: 25 minutes
Serving: 2
Ingredients:

- 1/4 cup hoisin sauce
- 1 tsp. garlic powder
- 1 tsp. onion powder
- 1/4 cup soy sauce
- 1/4 cup apple cider vinegar
- 1 lb. pork ribs

Directions:

1. In a mixing bowl, add all the ingredients. Combine the ingredients to mix well with each other.
2. Add the pork ribs and coat well. Refrigerate for 2 to 4 hours to marinate.
3. Take the Ninja Foodi Grill, arrange it over your kitchen platform, and open the top lid.
4. Arrange the grill grate and close the top lid.
5. Press "GRILL" and select the "MED" grill function. Adjust the timer to 24 minutes and then press "START/STOP." The Ninja Foodi will start preheating.
6. The Ninja Foodi is preheated and ready to cook when it starts beeping. After you hear a beep, open the top lid.
7. Arrange the pork ribs over the grill grate.
8. Close the top lid and cook for 12 minutes. Now open the top lid, flip the ribs.
9. Close the top lid and cook for 12 more minutes.
10. Serve them warm.

Nutrition:

- Calories: 326 Fat: 9 g
- Sat fat: 3 g Trans fat: 0 g
- Carbs: 26.5 g
- Fiber: 5 g
- Sodium: 529 mg
- Protein: 27 g

93. Bourbon Pork Chops

Preparation time: 5 to 10 minutes
Cooking time: 36 minutes
Serving: 4
Ingredients:

- 4 boneless pork chops
- Sea salt and ground black pepper to taste
- 1/4 cup apple cider vinegar
- 1/4 cup soy sauce
- 3 tbsp. Worcestershire sauce
- 2 cups ketchup - 3/4 cup bourbon
- 1 cup packed brown sugar
- 1/2 tbsp. dry mustard powder

Directions:

1. Take the Ninja Foodi Grill, arrange it over your kitchen platform, and open the top lid. Arrange the grill grate and close the top lid.
2. Press "grill" and select the "med" grill function. Adjust the timer to 16 minutes and then press "start/stop." The Ninja Foodi will start preheating. The Ninja Foodi is preheated and ready to cook when it starts beeping. After you hear a beep, open the top lid.
3. Arrange the pork chops over the grill grate.
4. Close the top lid and cook for 8 minutes. Now open the top lid, flip the pork chops.
5. Close the top lid and cook for 8 more minutes. Check the pork chops for doneness, cook for 2 more minutes if required.
6. In a saucepan, heat the soy sauce, sugar, ketchup, bourbon, vinegar, Worcestershire sauce, and mustard powder; stir-cook until boils.
7. Reduce heat and simmer for 20 minutes to thicken the sauce.
8. Season the pork chops with salt and black pepper. Serve them warm with the prepared sauce.

Nutrition:

- Calories: 346 Fat: 13.5 g
- Sat fat: 4 g Trans fat: 0 g
- Carbs: 27 g Fiber: 0.5 g
- Sodium: 1324 mg Protein: 27 g.

94. Grilled Pork Chops

Preparation time: 10 minutes
Cooking time: 15 minutes
Serving: 4
Ingredients:

- 4 pork chops
- Barbecue sauce to taste
- Salt and pepper to taste

Directions:

1. Add the grill grate to your Ninja Foodi Grill.
2. Set it to "grill." Close the hood.
3. Preheat at high for 15 minutes.
4. Season pork chops with salt and pepper.
5. Add to the grill grates.
6. Grill for 8 minutes.
7. Flip and cook for another 7 minutes, brushing both sides with barbecue sauce.

Nutrition:

- Calories: 368
- Fat: 19 g
- Carbs: 16 g
- Fiber: 5 g
- Protein: 23 g

95. Cuban Pork Chops

Preparation time: 8 hours and 20 minutes
Cooking time: 15 minutes
Serving: 4
Ingredients:

- 4 pork chops
- 1/2 cup olive oil
- 1/2 cup lime juice
- 1 tsp. orange zest
- 8 garlic cloves, minced
- 1/4 cup mint leaves, chopped
- 2 tsp. dried oregano
- 1 cup orange juice
- 1 tsp. lime zest
- 2 tsp. ground cumin
- 1 cup cilantro, chopped

Directions:

1. Place pork chops on a shallow plate.
2. In another bowl, mix the remaining ingredients.
3. Add the mixture to the pork chops.
4. Cover and marinate in the refrigerator for 8 hours.
5. Add the grill grate to the Ninja Foodi Grill. Seal the hood.
6. Choose the grill setting.
7. Set it to High.
8. Set the time to 15 minutes.
9. Close the hood and cook for 15 minutes, flipping once.
10. Serve it and enjoy.

Nutrition:

- Calories: 368
- Fat: 19 g
- Carbs: 16 g
- Fiber: 5 g
- Protein: 23 g

96. Ranch Pork Chops

Preparation time: 20 minutes
Cooking time: 20 minutes
Serving: 4
Ingredients:

- 1 tsp. garlic powder
- 1 tbsp. Parmesan cheese, grated
- 1/2 cup ranch dressing
- Salt and pepper to taste
- 1 cup breadcrumbs
- 1 tbsp. buttermilk
- 4 pork chops

Directions:

1. Mix garlic powder, breadcrumbs, Parmesan cheese, salt, and pepper in a bowl.
2. Combine buttermilk and ranch dressing in another bowl.
3. Dip the pork chops in the buttermilk mixture.
4. Dredge with the breadcrumb mixture.
5. Set the Ninja Foodi Grill to Air Fryer.
6. Cook at 330°F for 10 minutes per side.

Nutrition:

- Calories: 368
- Fat: 19 g
- Carbs: 16 g
- Fiber: 5 g
- Protein: 23 g

97. Chili Pork Ribs

Preparation time: 5 to 10 minutes
Cooking time: 60 minutes
Serving: 6
Ingredients:
Sauce:

- 1/2 cup soy sauce
- 1/6 cup lemon juice
- 1/2 cup packed brown sugar
- 1/3 cup ketchup
- 3/4 tsp. minced gingerroot

Ribs:

- 3 lb. pork baby back ribs
- 1 tbsp. chili powder
- 1 tsp. garlic powder
- 1 1/2 tsp. cumin, ground
- 1 tbsp. paprika powder
- Salt to taste
- 1 1/2 tbsp. sugar, brown

Directions:
1. In a mixing bowl, add the spices and sugar. Combine the ingredients to mix well with each other.
2. Add the ribs and rub evenly. Cover and refrigerate for about 1 hour to marinate.
3. In a saucepan, heat all the sauce ingredients for about 8 minutes. Set it aside.
4. Take the Ninja Foodi Grill, arrange it over your kitchen platform, and open the top lid.
5. Arrange the grill grate and close the top lid.
6. Press "grill" and select the "high" grill function. Adjust the timer to 45 minutes and then press "start/stop." Ninja Foodi will start preheating.
7. The Ninja Foodi is preheated and ready to cook when it starts beeping. After you hear a beep, open the top lid. Arrange the ribs over the grill grate.
8. Close the top lid and cook for 10 minutes. Now open the top lid, flip the ribs. Close the top lid and cook for ten more minutes. Keep flipping every 10 minutes.
9. Serve them warm with the prepared sauce.

Nutrition:
- Calories: 362 Fat: 19 g
- Sat fat: 4.5 g Trans fat: 0 g
- Carbs: 32.5 g Fiber: 1.5 g
- Sodium: 625 mg Protein: 22 g.

98. Breaded Pork Chop

Preparation time: 7 minutes
Cooking time: 12 minutes
Serving: 4
Ingredients:

- 4 (5-oz.) 3/4" boneless pork chops, fat trimmed
- 1/2 cup panko bread crumbs
- 2 tbsp. parmesan cheese, grated
- 1 egg, beaten
- 1 tsp. paprika
- 1/2 tsp. garlic powder
- 1/2 tsp. onion powder
- Salt and pepper to taste

Directions:
1. Preheat the Ninja Air Fryer to 400°F and spray the air fryer basket with nonstick spray.
2. Combine the panko bread crumbs, parmesan cheese, salt, pepper, onion, powder, garlic powder, and paprika in a shallow bowl large enough to fit the pork chops.
3. Place the egg in another bowl of the same size.
4. Dip the pork chops into the egg and coat them with the panko mixture
5. Place the pork chops into the air fryer and cook for 12 minutes. Flip halfway through the process.
6. Serve it with your favorite sides.

Nutrition:
- Calories: 304
- Carbs: 11.7 g
- Fat: 15.6 g
- Protein: 29.5 g.

99. Italian Herb Pork Chops

Preparation time: 4 minutes
Cooking time: 12 minutes
Serving: 2
Ingredients:

- 2 1" thick pork chops
- 1/2 tbsp. Italian seasoning
- 2 tbsp. olive oil

Directions:

1. Combine all the ingredients and allow to marinate in a sealed plastic bag for at least 2 hours.
2. Preheat the Air Fryer to 350°F.
3. Place the pork chops in the air fryer basket and cook for 12 minutes. Flip halfway through the cooking process.
4. Allow the pork chops to sit for at least 5 minutes before serving.

Nutrition:

- Calories: 387
- Carbs: 0.4 g
- Fat: 34.9 g
- Protein: 18 g

100. Italian Stuffed Pork Chops

Preparation time: 10 minutes
Cooking time: 12 minutes
Serving: 4
Ingredients:

- 4 thick-cut pork chops
- 4 tbsp. cream cheese
- 1 cup spinach
- 1/2 cup mozzarella cheese
- 1/2 tbsp. dried rosemary
- 1/2 tbsp. dried oregano
- 1/2 tbsp. garlic powder
- 1/2 tbsp. onion powder
- 1 tsp. paprika
- Salt and pepper to taste

Directions:

1. Preheat the Ninja Air Fryer to 400°F.
2. Butterfly the pork chops using a sharp knife. Season with salt and pepper.
3. Add all the remaining ingredients to a small bowl and combine thoroughly.
4. Fill each pork chop with an equal amount of filling.
5. Place the pork chops filling side up in the air fryer and cook for up to 12 minutes. Serve them with the desired sides.

Nutrition:

- Calories: 378
- Carbs: 3.1 g
- Fat: 19.4 g
- Protein: 23.4 g.

101. Roast Beef With Garlic

Preparation time: 15 minutes
Cooking time: 1 hour and 10 minutes
Serving: 4
Ingredients:

- 2 lb. beef roast, sliced
- 2 tbsp. vegetable oil
- Salt and pepper to taste
- 6 garlic cloves

Directions:

1. Coat the beef roast with oil.
2. Season with salt and pepper.
3. Place them inside the Ninja Foodi Grill pot.
4. Sprinkle garlic on top.
5. Choose the Bake setting.
6. Set it to 400°F and cook for 30 minutes.
7. Reduce the temperature to 375°F and cook for another 40 minutes.

Serving suggestions: Serve with mashed potato and gravy.
Preparation/cooking tips: If refrigerated, let beef come to room temperature 2 hours before cooking.
Nutrition:

- Calories: 390
- Fat: 29 g
- Carbs: 5 g
- Protein: 20 g

102. Grilled Steak and Potatoes

Preparation time: 20 minutes
Cooking time: 50 minutes
Serving: 4
Ingredients:

- 4 potatoes
- 3 sirloin steaks
- 1/4 cup avocado oil
- 2 tbsp. steak seasoning
- Salt to taste

Directions:

1. Poke the potatoes with a fork.
2. Coat them with half of the avocado oil.
3. Season with salt.
4. Add to the air fryer basket.
5. Choose the air fry function in your Ninja Foodi Grill.
6. Seal the hood and cook at 400°F for 35 minutes.
7. Flip and cook for another 10 minutes.
8. Transfer to a plate.
9. Add the grill grate to the Ninja Foodi Grill.
10. Season the steaks with sauce and add them to the grill grate.
11. Set it to High.
12. Cook for 7 minutes per side.
13. Serve steaks with potatoes.

Serving suggestions: Serve with steak sauce and hot sauce.
Preparation/cooking tips: Press steaks onto the grill to give it grill marks.
Nutrition:

- Calories: 245
- Fat: 26 g
- Carbs: 7 g
- Protein: 19 g

103. Authentic Korean Flank Steak

Preparation time: 10 minutes
Cooking time: 12 minutes
Serving: 4
Ingredients:

- 1 tsp. red pepper flakes
- 1/2 cup and 1 tbsp. soy sauce
- 1 1/2 lb. flank steak
- 1/4 cup and 2 tbsp. vegetable oil
- 1/2 cup rice wine vinegar
- 3 tbsp. sriracha
- 4 garlic cloves, minced
- 2 tbsp. ginger, minced
- 2 tbsp. honey
- 3 tbsp. sesame oil
- 1 tsp. sugar
- Salt to taste

Directions:

1. Take a bowl and add 1/2 cup of soy sauce, half of the rice wine, honey, ginger, garlic, 2 tbsp. of sriracha, 2 tbsp. of sesame oil, and vegetable oil.
2. Mix well, pour half of the mixture over the steak and rub well.
3. Cover the steak and let it sit for 10 minutes.
4. Prepare the salad mix by adding the remaining rice wine vinegar, sesame oil, sugar, red pepper flakes, sriracha sauce, soy sauce, and salt in a salad bowl.
5. Preheat your Ninja Foodi Grill on High with the timer set to 12 minutes.
6. Transfer the steak to your Grill and cook for 6 minutes per side.
7. Slice and then serve with the salad mix.
8. Enjoy!

Nutrition:

- Calories: 327 Fat: 4 g
- Sat fat: 0.5 g Carbs: 33 g
- Fiber: 1 g Sodium: 142 mg Protein: 24 g

104. Grilled Beef Burgers

Preparation time: 5 to 10 minutes
Cooking time: 10 minutes
Serving: 4
Ingredients:

- 4 oz. cream cheese
- 4 slices bacon, cooked and crumbled
- 2 seeded jalapeño peppers, stemmed, and minced
- 1/2 cup shredded Cheddar cheese
- 1/2 tsp. chili powder - 1/4 tsp. paprika
- 1/4 tsp. ground black pepper
- 2 lb. ground beef - 4 hamburger buns
- 4 slices pepper Jack cheese - **Optional—** Lettuce, sliced tomato, and sliced red onion

Directions:

1. In a mixing bowl, combine the peppers, Cheddar cheese, cream cheese, and bacon until well combined. Prepare the ground beef into 8 patties. Add the cheese mixture onto four of the patties; arrange a second patty on top of each to prepare four burgers. Press gently.
2. In another bowl, combine the chili powder, paprika, and pepper. Sprinkle the mixture onto the sides of the burgers. Take the Ninja Foodi Grill, arrange it over your kitchen platform, and open the top lid. Arrange the grill grate and close the top lid. Press "GRILL" and select the "HIGH" grill function. Adjust the timer to 4 minutes and then press "START/STOP." The Ninja Foodi will start preheating. The Ninja Foodi is preheated and ready to cook when it starts beeping. After you hear a beep, open the top lid. Arrange the burgers over the grill grate.
3. Close the top lid and allow it to cook for 10 minutes. Cook for 3 to 4 more minutes if needed.
4. Serve them warm with buns. Add your choice of toppings: pepper Jack cheese, lettuce, tomato, and red onion.

Nutrition:

- Calories: 783 Fat: 38 g Sat fat: 16 g
- Trans fat: 0 g Carbs: 25 g Fiber: 3 g
- Sodium: 1259 mg Protein: 57.5 g

105. Generous Pesto Beef Meal

Preparation time: 10 minutes
Cooking time: 14 minutes
Serving: 4
Ingredients:

- 1/2 tsp. pepper
- 1/2 tsp. salt
- 1/2 cup feta cheese, crumbled
- 2/3 cup pesto
- 1/2 cup walnuts, chopped
- 4 cup grape tomatoes, halved
- 4 cup penne pasta, uncooked
- 10 oz. baby spinach, chopped
- 4 beef (6 oz. each) tenderloin steaks

Directions:

1. Cook the pasta according to the package directions.
2. Drain the pasta and rinse it.
3. Keep the pasta on the side.
4. Season the tenderloin steaks with pepper and salt.
5. Preheat your Ninja Foodi Grill to High and set the timer to 7 minutes.
6. You will hear a beep once the preheating sequence is complete.
7. Transfer the steak to your grill and cook for 7 minutes, flip and cook for 7 more minutes.
8. Take a bowl and add pasta, walnuts, spinach, tomatoes, and pesto.
9. Mix well.
10. Garnish your steak with cheese and serve with the prepared sauce.
11. Enjoy!

Nutrition:

- Calories: 361 Fat: 5 g
- Sat fat: 1 g
- Carbs: 16 g
- Fiber: 4 g
- Sodium: 269 mg
- Protein: 33 g

106. Meatball Sandwiches With Mozzarella and Basil

Preparation time: 5 minutes
Cooking time: 10 minutes
Serving: 4
Ingredients:

- 12 frozen meatballs
- 8 slices mozzarella cheese
- 4 sub rolls, halved lengthwise
- 1/2 cup marinara sauce, warmed
- 12 fresh basil leaves

Directions:

1. Select the air fryer, set the temperature to 350°F, and the time to 10 minutes. Select start/stop to start preheating.
2. When the unit beeps to signify it has preheated, place the meatballs in the unit. Close the hood and cook for 5 minutes.
3. While the meatballs are cooking, place 2 slices of mozzarella cheese on each sub roll. Use a spoon to spread the marinara sauce on top of the mozzarella slices. Press 3 leaves of basil into the sauce on each roll.
4. When the meatballs are cooked, place them on the sandwich and serve them.

Nutrition:

- Calories: 537
- Fat: 27 g
- Sat fat: 13 g
- Cholesterol: 80 mg
- Sodium: 1243 mg
- Carbs: 46 g
- Fiber: 4 g
- Protein: 34 g

107. Soy and Garlic Steak Kebabs

Preparation time: 5 minutes
Cooking time: 12 minutes
Serving: 4
Ingredients:

- 3/4 cup soy sauce
- 5 garlic cloves, minced
- 3 tbsp. sesame oil
- 1/2 cup canola oil
- 1/3 cup sugar
- 1/4 tsp. dried ground ginger
- 2 (10 to 12 oz.) New York strip steaks, cut in 2-inch cubes
- 1 cup whole white mushrooms
- 1 red bell pepper, seeded, and cut into 2-inch cubes - 1 red onion, cut into 2-inch wedges

Directions:

1. In a medium bowl, whisk together the soy sauce, garlic, sesame oil, canola oil, sugar, and ginger until well combined. Add the steak and toss to coat. Cover and refrigerate for at least 30 minutes.
2. Insert the Grill Grate and close the hood. Select grill set the temperature to medium and set the time to 12 minutes. Select start/stop to start preheating.
3. While the unit is preheating, assemble the skewers in the following order: steak, mushroom, bell pepper, onion. Ensure the ingredients are pushed almost completely down to the end of the skewers. When the unit beeps to indicate it has preheated, place the skewers on the Grill Grate. Close the hood and cook for 8 minutes without flipping. After 8 minutes, check the steak for the desired doneness, cooking up to 4 more minutes if desired.

Nutrition:

- Calories: 647 Fat: 45 g
- Sat fat: 12 g Cholesterol: 135 mg
- Sodium: 1001 mg Carbs: 17 g
- Fiber: 1 g Protein: 47 g

108. Chili-Rubbed Flank Steak

Preparation time: 10 minutes
Cooking time: 8 minutes
Serving: 2
Ingredients:

- 1 tbsp. chili powder
- 1 tsp. dried oregano
- 2 tsp. ground cumin
- 1 tsp. sea salt
- 1/4 tsp. freshly ground black pepper
- 2 (8 oz.) flank steaks

Directions:

1. Insert the Grill Grate and close the hood. Select grill set the temperature to high and set the time to 8 minutes. Select start/stop to start preheating.
2. In a small bowl, mix the chili powder, oregano, cumin, salt, and pepper. Use your hands to rub the spice mixture on all sides of the steaks.
3. When the unit beeps to indicate it has preheated, place the steaks on the Grill Grate. Gently press the steaks down to maximize grill marks. Close the hood and cook for 4 minutes. After 4 minutes, flip the steaks, close the hood and cook for 4 more minutes.
4. Remove the steaks from the grill and transfer them to a cutting board. Let them rest for 5 minutes before slicing and serving.

Nutrition:

- Calories: 363
- Fat: 15 g
- Sat fat: 6 g
- Cholesterol: 100 mg
- Sodium: 1008 mg
- Carbs: 4 g
- Fiber: 2 g
- Protein: 51 g

109. Beef Bulgogi

Preparation time: 5 minutes
Cooking time: 5 minutes
Serving: 4
Ingredients:

- 1/3 cup soy sauce
- 2 tbsp. sesame oil
- 21/2 tbsp. brown sugar
- 3 garlic cloves, minced
- 1/2 tsp. freshly ground black pepper
- 1 lb. rib-eye steak, thinly sliced
- 2 scallions, thinly sliced, for garnish
- Toasted sesame seeds, for garnish

Directions:

1. In a small bowl, whisk together the soy sauce, sesame oil, brown sugar, garlic, and black pepper until fully combined.
2. Place the beef into a large shallow bowl and pour the sauce over the slices. Cover and refrigerate for 1 hour.
3. Insert the Grill Grate and close the hood. Select grill set the temperature to medium and the time to 5 minutes. Select start/stop to start preheating.
4. When the unit beeps to indicate it has preheated, place the beef onto the Grill Grate. Close the hood and cook for 4 minutes without flipping.
5. After 4 minutes, check the steak for the desired doneness, cooking for up to 1 more minute if desired.
6. Garnish with the scallion and sesame seeds and serve them.

Nutrition:

- Calories: 403
- Fat: 31 g
- Sat fat: 13 g
- Cholesterol: 76 mg
- Sodium: 1263 mg
- Carbs: 8 g
- Fiber: 0 g
- Protein: 22 g

110. Grilled Steak Salad With Blue Cheese Dressing

Preparation time: 5 minutes
Cooking time: 16 minutes
Serving: 4 to 6
Ingredients:

- 4 (8 oz.) skirt steaks
- Sea salt to taste
- Freshly ground black pepper to taste
- 6 cups chopped romaine lettuce
- 3/4 cup cherry tomatoes halved
- 1/4 cup blue cheese, crumbled
- 2 avocados, peeled and sliced
- 1 cup blue cheese dressing

Directions:

1. Insert the Grill Grate and close the hood. Select grill set the temperature to high and set the time to 8 minutes. Select start/stop to start preheating.
2. Season the steaks on both sides with salt and pepper.
3. When the unit beeps to indicate it has preheated, place 2 steaks on the Grill Grate. Gently press the steaks down to maximize grill marks. Close the hood and cook for 4 minutes. After 4 minutes, flip the steaks, close the hood and cook for an additional 4 minutes.
4. Remove the steaks from the grill and transfer to them a cutting board. Tent with aluminum foil.
5. Repeat step 3 with the remaining 2 steaks.
6. When the meat is ready, serve it with romaine salad, cherry tomatoes avocado, and cheese.

Nutrition:

- Calories: 911
- Fat: 67 g
- Sat fat: 18 g
- Cholesterol: 167 mg
- Sodium: 1062 mg
- Carbs: 22 g
- Fiber: 7 g
- Protein: 56 g

111. Beef Sirloin Roast

Preparation time: 10 minutes
Cooking time: 50 minutes
Serving: 8
Ingredients:

- 1 tbsp. smoked paprika
- 1 tsp. ground cumin
- 1 tsp. garlic powder
- Salt and ground black pepper, as required
- 2 1/2 lb. sirloin roast

Directions:

1. In a bowl, mix the spices, salt, and black pepper.
2. Rub the roast with spice mixture generously.
3. Place the sirloin roast into the greased baking pan.
4. Press the "Power Button" of the Ninja Foodi Grill and select the "Roast" mode.
5. Press the Time button and again turn the dial to set the cooking time to 50 minutes.
6. Set the temperature at 350°F.
7. Press the "Start/Pause" button to start.
8. When the unit beeps to show that it is preheated, open the lid and insert the baking pan in the unit.
9. Remove the baking pan from the unit and place the roast onto a platter for about 10 minutes before slicing.
10. With a sharp knife, cut the beef roast into desired-sized slices and serve them.

Nutrition:

- Calories: 260
- Fat: 11.9 g
- Sat fat: 4.4 g
- Cholesterol: 101 mg
- Sodium: 98 mg
- Carbs: 0.4 g
- Fiber: 0.1 g
- Sugar: 0.1 g
- Protein: 38 g

112. Simple Beef Tenderloin

Preparation time: 10 minutes
Cooking time: 50 minutes
Serving: 10
Ingredients:

- 1 (3 1/2 lb.) beef tenderloin, trimmed
- 2 tbsp. olive oil
- Salt and ground black pepper, as required

Directions:

1. With kitchen twine, tie the tenderloin.
2. Rub the tenderloin with oil and season with salt and black pepper.
3. Place the tenderloin into the greased baking pan.
4. Press the "Power Button" of the Ninja Foodi Grill and select the "Roast" mode.
5. Press the Time button and again turn the dial to set the cooking time to 50 minutes.
6. Set the temperature at 400°F.
7. Press the "Start/Pause" button to start.
8. When the unit beeps to show that it is preheated, open the lid and insert the baking pan in the unit.
9. Remove it from the unit and place the tenderloin onto a platter for about 10 minutes before slicing.
10. With a sharp knife, cut the tenderloin into desired-sized slices and serve.

Nutrition:

- Calories: 351
- Fat: 17.3 g
- Sat fat: 5.9 g
- Cholesterol: 146 mg
- Sodium: 109 mg
- Carbs: 0 g
- Fiber: 0 g
- Sugar: 0 g
- Protein: 46 g

113. Beef Chuck Roast

Preparation time: 10 minutes
Cooking time: 45 minutes
Serving: 6
Ingredients:

- 1 (2 lb.) beef chuck roast
- 1 tbsp. olive oil
- 1 tsp. dried rosemary, crushed
- 1 tsp. dried thyme, crushed
- Salt, as required

Directions:

1. In a bowl, add the oil, herbs, and salt and mix well.
2. Coat the beef roast with the herb mixture generously.
3. Arrange the beef roast onto the greased cooking pan.
4. Press the "Power Button" of the Ninja Foodi Grill and select the "Air Fryer" mode.
5. Set the cooking time to 45 minutes.
6. Set the temperature at 360°F.
7. Press the "Start/Pause" button to start.
8. When the unit beeps to show that it is preheated, open the lid and insert the baking pan in the unit and cook it.
9. Remove from the unit and place the roast onto a cutting board.
10. With a piece of foil, cover the beef roast for about 20 minutes before slicing.
11. With a sharp knife, cut the beef roast into desired-sized slices and serve them.

Nutrition:

- Calories: 304 Fat: 14 g
- Sat fat: 4.5 g
- Cholesterol: 130 mg
- Sodium: 82 mg
- Carbs: 0.2 g
- Fiber: 0.2 g
- Sugar: 0 g
- Protein: 41.5 g

114. Filet Mignon With Pineapple Salsa

Preparation time: 15 minutes
Cooking time: 8 minutes
Serving: 4
Ingredients:

- 4 (6 to 8 oz.) filet mignon steaks
- 1 tbsp. canola oil, divided - Sea salt to taste
- Freshly ground black pepper to taste
- 1/2 medium pineapple, cored and diced
- 1 medium red onion, diced
- 1 jalapeño pepper, seeded, stemmed, and diced
- 1 tbsp. freshly squeezed lime juice
- 1/4 cup chopped fresh cilantro leaves
- Chili powder to taste - Ground coriander to taste

Directions:

1. Rub each filet on all sides with 1/2 tbsp. of oil; then season with salt and pepper.
2. Insert the Grill Grate and close the hood. Select grill set the temperature to high and set the time to 8 minutes. Select start/stop to start preheating.
3. Combine pineapple, jalapeño pepper, red onion, cilantro, lime juice, chili powder, and salt in a small bowl for the salsa. Set it aside.
4. When the unit beeps to indicate it has preheated, add the filets to the Grill Grate. Gently press the filets down to maximize grill marks. Then close the hood. After 4 minutes, open the hood and flip the filets. Close the hood and continue cooking for an additional 4 minutes or until the filets' internal temperature reads 125°F on a food thermometer. Remove the filets from the grill; they will continue to cook (called carry-over cooking) to a food-safe temperature even after you've removed them from the grill.
5. Let the filets rest for a total of 10 minutes. This allows the natural juices to redistribute into the steak. Top the filets with sauce and serve.

Nutrition:

- Calories: 571 Fat: 25 g Sat fat: 8 g
- Cholesterol: 192 mg Sodium: 264 mg Carbs: 20 g
- Fiber: 3 g Protein: 65 g

115. Gochujang-Marinated Baby Back Ribs

Preparation time: 10 minutes
Cooking time: 22 minutes
Serving: 4
Ingredients:

- 1/4 cup gochujang paste
- 1/4 cup soy sauce
- 1/4 cup freshly squeezed orange juice
- 2 tbsp. apple cider vinegar
- 2 tbsp. sesame oil
- 6 garlic cloves, minced
- 1 1/2 tbsp. brown sugar
- 1 tbsp. grated fresh ginger
- 1 tsp. salt
- 4 (8 to 10 oz.) baby back ribs

Directions:

1. In a medium bowl, add the gochujang paste, soy sauce, orange juice, vinegar, oil, garlic, sugar, ginger, and salt, and stir to combine.
2. Place the baby's back ribs on a baking sheet and coat all sides with the sauce. Cover with aluminum foil and refrigerate for 6 hours.
3. Insert the Grill Grate and close the hood. Select grill set the temperature to medium and set the time to 22 minutes. Select start/stop to start preheating.
4. When the unit beeps to indicate it has preheated, place the ribs on the Grill Grate. Close the hood and cook for 11 minutes. Then flip the ribs, close the hood and cook for an additional 11 minutes.

Nutrition:

- Calories: 826
- Fat: 64 g
- Sat fat: 22 g
- Cholesterol: 191 mg
- Sodium: 2113 mg
- Carbs: 19 g
- Fiber: 1 g
- Protein: 41 g

116. Glazed Lamb Chops

Preparation time: 10 minutes
Cooking time: 15 minutes
Serving: 4
Ingredients:

- 1 tbsp. Dijon mustard
- 1/2 tbsp. fresh lime juice
- 1 tsp. honey
- 1/2 tsp. olive oil
- Salt and ground black pepper to taste
- 4 (4 oz.) lamb loin chops

Directions:

1. In a large bowl, mix the mustard, lemon juice, oil, honey, salt, and black pepper.
2. Add the chops and coat them with the mixture generously.
3. Place the chops onto the greased "Sheet Pan."
4. Press the "Power Button" of the Ninja Foodi Grill and turn the dial to select the "Bake" mode.
5. Press the Time button and again turn the dial to set the cooking time to 15 minutes.
6. Now push the Temp button and rotate the dial to set the temperature at 390°F.
7. Press the "Start/Pause" button to start.
8. When the unit beeps to show that it is preheated, open the lid.
9. Insert the "Sheet Pan" in the unit.
10. Flip the chops once halfway through.
11. Serve them hot.

Nutrition:

- Calories: 224
- Fat: 9.1 g
- Sat fat: 3.1 g
- Cholesterol: 102 mg
- Sodium: 169 mg
- Carbs: 1.7 g
- Fiber: 0.1 g
- Sugar: 1.5 g
- Protein: 32 g

117. Buttered Leg of Lamb

Preparation time: 15 minutes
Cooking time: 1 1/4 hours
Serving: 8
Ingredients:

- 1 (2 1/4-lb.) boneless leg of lamb
- 3 tbsp. butter, melted
- Salt and ground black pepper, as required
- 4 fresh rosemary sprigs

Directions:

1. Rub the leg of lamb with butter and sprinkle with salt and black pepper.
2. Wrap the leg of lamb with rosemary sprigs.
3. Press the "Power Button" of the Ninja Foodi Grill and select the "Air Fryer" mode.
4. Press the Time button and again turn the dial to set the cooking time to 75 minutes.
5. Now push the Temp button and set the temperature at 300°F.
6. Press the "Start/Pause" button to start.
7. When the unit beeps to show it is preheated, open the lid and arrange the leg of lamb into the unit.
8. Once cooked, remove from the unit and place the leg of lamb onto a cutting board for about 10 minutes before slicing it.
9. Cut into desired sized pieces and serve them.

Nutrition:

- Calories: 278
- Fat: 13.8 g
- Sat fat: 6.1 g
- Cholesterol: 126 mg
- Sodium: 147 mg
- Carbs: 0.5 g
- Fiber: 0.4 g
- Sugar: 0 g
- Protein: 35.9 g

118. Simple Lamb Chop

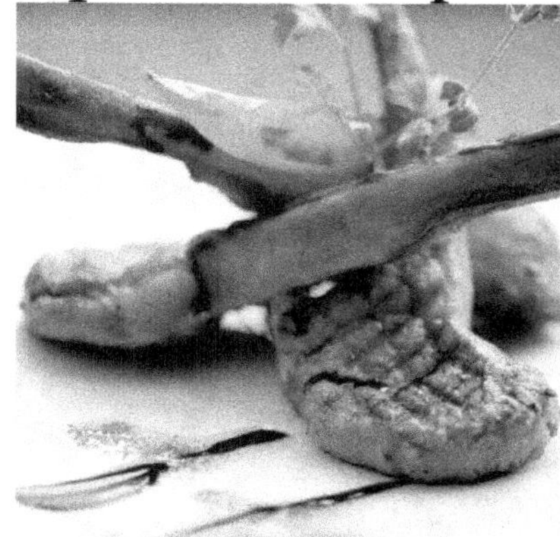

Preparation time: 5 minutes
Cooking time: 25 minutes
Serving: 2
Ingredients:

- 2 medium lamb chops
- 1 tbsp. lemon juice
- 1 tsp. dried rosemary
- 1 tsp. dried thyme
- Salt and pepper to taste

Directions:

1. Select "Air Fryer" mode. Preheat the Ninja Foodi to 350°F.
2. Combine all the ingredients to season the lamb chops thoroughly.
3. Place the lamb chops in the air fryer basket for 25 minutes.
4. Allow the lamb chops to rest for 10 minutes before serving.

Nutrition:

- Calories: 265
- Carbs: 5.9 g
- Fat: 15.2 g
- Protein: 25.2 g

119. Herbed Rack of Lamb

Preparation time: 7 minutes
Cooking time: 10 minutes
Serving: 4
Ingredients:

- 1 rack of lamb
- 3 tbsp. olive oil
- 1 tbsp. dried rosemary
- 1 tbsp. dried thyme
- 2 garlic cloves, minced
- Salt and pepper to taste

Directions:

1. Select "Air fryer." Preheat the Ninja Foodi to 360°F.
2. Combine all the ingredients, except the rack of lamb in a small bowl to form the seasoning.
3. Rub the mixture all over the rack of lamb and place it into the air fryer basket. Cook for 10 minutes and check the internal temperature. For rare meat, the internal temperature should be 145°F. For medium meat, the internal temperature should be 160°F. For well-done meat, the internal temperature should be 170°F.
4. Serve with your favorite sides after the lamb has rested for a minimum of 10 minutes.

Nutrition:

- Calories: 287
- Carbs: 1.5 g
- Fat: 20.7 g
- Protein: 23.2 g

120. Leg of Lamb

Preparation time: 5 minutes
Cooking time: 40 minutes
Serving: 5
Ingredients:

- 1 leg of lamb
- Salt and pepper to taste

Directions:

1. Select "Air Fryer." Preheat the Ninja Foodi Grill to 360°F.
2. Season the leg of lamb with salt and pepper, then place it in the air fryer basket. Cook for 40 minutes.
3. Serve it warm with desired sides.

Nutrition:

- Calories: 243 Carbs: 0 g
- Fat: 9.6 gProtein: 36 g

121. Crazy Greek Lamb Gyros

Preparation time: 10 minutes
Cooking time: 25 minutes
Serving: 8
Ingredients:

- 8 garlic cloves - 1 1/2 tsp. salt
- 2 lb. lamb meat, ground
- 2 tsp. rosemary - 1/2 tsp. pepper
- 1 small onion, chopped
- 2 tsp. ground marjoram

Directions:

1. Add onions, garlic, marjoram, rosemary, salt, and pepper to a food processor.
2. Process until combined well, add the ground lamb meat, and process again.
3. Press the meat mixture gently into a loaf pan.
4. Transfer the pan to your Ninja Foodi pot.
5. Lock the lid and select the "Bake" mode.
6. Bake for 25 minutes at 375°F.
7. Transfer to a serving dish and enjoy!

Nutrition:

- Calories: 242 Fat: 15 g
- Carbs: 2.4 g Protein: 21 g

CHAPTER 7:

~ 78 ~

Vegetable And Sides

122. Sweet Potato Fingers

Preparation time: 15 minutes
Cooking time: 20 minutes
Serving: 2
Ingredients:

- 1 cup Panko breadcrumbs
- 1/2 tsp. salt
- 1 lb. sweet potatoes, peeled and sliced
- 250 ml of Aquafaba

Directions:

1. Preheat the ninja Foodi grill by selecting AIR CRISP mode for 3 minutes at 375°F and close the hood.
2. Select START/PAUSE to begin the preheating process.
3. In a mixing bowl, combine breadcrumbs and salt.
4. Coat the sweet potato slices first with the Aquafaba then put them in the breadcrumb mixture.
5. Place it inside the crisper basket, avoid overlapping.
6. Air Crisp for 20 minutes at 375°F.
7. Once done, serve and enjoy.

Nutrition:

- Calories: 413
- Fat: 2.1 g
- Sodium: 1030 mg
- Carbs: 87.7 g
- Fiber: 16.3 g
- Sugar: 2.3 g
- Protein: 10.4 g

123. Mexican Street Corn

Preparation time: minutes
Cooking time: minutes
Serving: 2
Ingredients:

- 2 ears corn, shucked
- 1 tbsp. canola oil, divided
- Salt and black pepper, to taste

Sauce ingredients:

- 1 cup Cottage cheese, grated
- 1/4 cup mayonnaise
- 1/4 cup sour cream
- 1 lime, juiced
- 1/2 tsp. garlic powder
- 1/2 tsp. onion powder
- 1/8 cup fresh cilantro, chopped

Directions:

1. Insert grill grate in the ninja Foodi grill.
2. Close the hood and preheat it at MAX for 10 minutes.
3. Meanwhile, brush the corn with canola oil and season it with salt and black pepper.
4. Once the unit is preheated grill the corn inside the unit for 7 minutes.
5. Afterward, flip the corns and then grill for 5 more minutes.
6. Meanwhile, mix all the sauce ingredients in a mixing bowl.
7. Once the corn is cooked serve it with sauce.

Nutrition:

- Calories: 476
- Fat: 26.3 g
- Sodium: 707 mg
- Carbs: 42.2 g
- Fiber: 4.3 g
- Sugar: 7.7 g
- Protein: 21.6 g

124. Honey and Herb Charred Carrots

Preparation time: 10 minutes
Cooking time: 6 minutes
Serving: 2
Ingredients:

- 2 tsp. honey
- 4 tsp. melted butter
- Salt, to taste
- 6 medium carrots
- 1 tbsp. fresh parsley, chopped
- 1 tbsp. rosemary, chopped

Directions:

1. First, insert the grill grate in the ninja Foodi grill and select the grill function
2. Set the time to MAX for 10 minutes, by selecting the grill function.
3. Select start to begin preheating.
4. Meanwhile in a small bowl add honey, salt, and melted butter.
5. Whisk the ingredients all well.
6. Coat the carrots with the honey butter and then rub them with the listed herbs.
7. When the unit beeps and preheating is done, add the carrots to the cooking basket of the unit.
8. Close the hood and set it to MAX for 6 minutes at the grill mode.
9. Once done, serve.

Nutrition:

- Calories: 170
- Fat: 7.9 g
- Sodium: 260 mg
- Carbs: 25 g
- Fiber: 5.3 g
- Sugar: 14.8 g
- Protein: 1.7 g

125. Roasted Cauliflower

Preparation time: 20 minutes
Cooking time: 10 minutes
Serving: 2
Ingredients:

- 1/2 head white cauliflower, cut in florets
- 1/2 head purple cauliflower, cut into florets
- 2 tbsp. extra virgin olive oil
- Salt and black pepper, to taste

Sauce ingredients:

- 2 tbsp. Asian chili paste
- 1/4 cup extra virgin olive oil
- 2 tbsp. rice wine vinegar
- 3 tbsp. maple syrup
- 1 tbsp. coconut amino
- 1/4 cup roasted peanuts
- 1 tbsp. sesame seeds

Directions:

1. Add the crisper basket to the ninja grill and close the hood.
2. Select the AIR CRISP mode and set the time to 25 minutes at 375°F.
3. Next, take a bowl and combine cauliflower with oil, salt, and pepper.
4. Toss it to coat it finely.
5. Once the unit has preheated and the timer beep adds the cauliflower to the basket.
6. Let it air crisp for 10 minutes.
7. Meanwhile, mix all sauce ingredients in a large mixing bowl.
8. Once cauliflower is done serve it with sauce.

Nutrition:

- Calories: 534
- Fat: 47 g
- Sodium: 40 mg
- Carbs: 29.4 g
- Fiber: 3.1 g
- Sugar: 19.6 g
- Protein: 6.5 g

126. Grilled Tomato Salsa

Preparation time: 20 minutes
Cooking time: 10 minutes
Serving: 2
Ingredients:

- 6 Roma tomatoes cut in half lengthwise
- 1/2 red onion, peeled, cut in quarters
- 2 jalapeño peppers, cut in half, seeds removed
- Salt and black pepper, to taste
- 2 tbsp. canola oil
- 1 bunch cilantro stems trimmed
- 3 garlic cloves, peeled
- 2 tbsp. ground cumin
- 1 tsp. lime zest
- 3 limes, juiced

Directions:

1. Take a bowl and add onion, jalapeno, tomatoes, salt, canola oil, and black pepper.
2. Mix it very well.
3. First, insert the grill grate in the ninja food grill and select the grill function
4. Set the time to MAX for 10 minutes, by selecting the grill function.
5. Select start to begin preheating.
6. After the preheating is done, place the vegetable mixture from the bowl on the grill grate.
7. Close the hood and cook for 5 minutes.
8. After 5 minutes open the unit and flip the vegetables let it grill for 5 more minutes.
9. Once the grilling is one, transfer the ingredients from the unit to the food processor.
10. Add in the remaining listed ingredients as well, and pulse to form a salsa.
11. Once the salsa is prepared, serve and enjoy.

Nutrition:

- Calories: 235 Fat: 16.2 g
- Sodium: 30 mg
- Carbs: 22.1 g
- Fiber: 6.3 g
- Sugar: 11.6 g
- Protein: 5.1 g

127. Eggplant With Greek Yogurt

Preparation time: 18 minutes
Cooking time: 10 minutes
Serving: 1
Ingredients:

- 1 large eggplant, sliced
- 2 tbsp. olive oil
- 1 cup Greek yogurt
- 1 tsp. sweet paprika
- Salt and black pepper, to taste
- 1 lime cut in half

Directions:

1. Season the eggplant with salt and let it sit for 30 minutes to remove the bitterness.
2. Wash and pat dry the eggplants.
3. First, insert the grill grate in the ninja food grill and select the grill function.
4. Set the time to MAX for 10 minutes, by selecting the grill function.
5. Select start to begin preheating.
6. Season the eggplants with paprika, pepper, oil add lime juice.
7. Once preheating is done, add the eggplants to the Grill Grate and close the hood.
8. Select the GRILL function and set the temperature to the MAX setting.
9. Let it grill for 8 to 10 minutes.
10. Once done, serve the eggplants with a dollop of Greek yogurt.

Nutrition:

- Calories: 1288
- Fat: 53.4 g
- Sodium: 404 mg
- Carbs: 83 g
- Fiber: 19 g
- Sugar: 63.5 g
- Protein: 126.6 g

128. Stuffed Jalapeno

Preparation time: 15 minutes
Cooking time: 5 minutes
Serving: 1
Ingredients:

- 2 eggs, whisked
- 1 cup cottage cheese
- 1 cup almond flour
- 4 jalapenos, cut lengthwise and seeds removed
- 1/4 tsp. garlic powder
- 1/4 tsp. onion powder
- 1/4 tsp. Cajun seasoning
- Black pepper and salt, to taste
- Oil spray

Directions:

1. Put the Crisper Basket inside the unit.
2. Then close the hood.
3. Select AIR CRISP, at 400°F, for 5 minutes.
4. Select the start to begin preheating.
5. Mix all dry spice ingredients in a bowl.
6. Whisk eggs in another bowl.
7. Fill the cavity of jalapeño with cheese, and then dip it in egg wash then coat it with flour mixture.
8. Add the jalapenos to the Air Crisper basket ad grease it with oil spray.
9. Air crisp at 350°F, for 5 minutes.
10. Once done, serve.

Nutrition:

- Calories: 517
- Fat: 28 g
- Sodium: 2425 mg
- Carbs: 20 g
- Fiber: 5.4 g
- Sugar: 4.7 g
- Protein: 50 g

129. Parmesan, Cheddar, and Zucchini Casserole

Preparation time: 20 minutes
Cooking time: 30 minutes
Serving: 4
Ingredients:

- 1 egg, whisked
- 6 saltine crackers, or as needed, crushed
- 3 tbsp. bread crumbs
- 1 lb. yellow squash, sliced
- 1 lb. zucchini, sliced
- 1/2 cup Cheddar cheese
- 1/2 cup of parmesan cheese
- 1/2 onion, diced
- 1/2 cup biscuit baking mix
- 1/2 cup butter
- Oil spray, for greasing

Directions:

1. Take a crisper basket and grease it with oil spray, and place it inside the ninja Foodi grill.
2. Select AIR CRISP mode and set it to 10 minutes at 350°F.
3. Let the preheating begin.
4. Take a bowl and add zucchini, yellow squash, and onion and add it to the crisper basket once preheating is done.
5. Cook it for 15 minutes, at 360°F, or until tender.
6. Take a bowl and whisk eggs in it along with butter, baking mix, parmesan, and cheddar cheese.
7. Pour it over vegetables in a basket and then top it with cracker and bread crumbs.
8. Let it air crisp for 15 minutes at 390°F.
9. Once done, serve and enjoy.

Nutrition:

- Calories: 513
- Fat: 38.2 g
- Sodium: 989 mg
- Carbs: 23.5 g
- Fiber: 2.9 g
- Sugar: 6.2 g
- Protein: 17.8 g

130. Artichokes With Honey Dijon

Preparation time: 15 minutes
Cooking time: 15 minutes
Serving: 2
Ingredients:

- 6 whole artichokes
- 1/2 gallon water
- Sea salt to taste
- Olive oil to taste
- 1/4 cup raw honey
- 1/4 cup boiling water
- 3 tbsp. Dijon mustard

Directions:

1. Cut the artichokes lengthwise in half.
2. Simmer artichokes in water and salt mixture for 20 minutes.
3. First, insert the grill grate in the ninja food grill and select the grill function.
4. Set the time to MAX for 8 minutes, buy selecting grill function.
5. Select start to begin preheating.
6. Remove the artichokes from the water.
7. Pat dry and then drizzle it with olive oil and salt.
8. Once the unit is preheated grill artichokes by placing them on the grill grate for 15 minutes at MAX.
9. Remember to flip the artichokes halfway through.
10. Mix the honey, boiled water, and Dijon in a bowl.
11. Baste the artichokes with the mixture until they absorb the mixture.
12. Once done, serve and enjoy.

Nutrition:

- Calories: 145
- Fat: 0.9 g
- Sodium: 416 mg
- Carbs: 36.5 g
- Fiber: 1 g
- Sugar: 35 g
- Protein: 1.3 g

131. Garlic and Sage Tomatoes

Preparation time: 10 minutes
Cooking time: 6 minutes
Serving: 2
Ingredients:

- 1/2 tbsp. sage, chopped
- 6 plum tomatoes
- 1 tbsp. olive oil
- Salt and black pepper, to taste
- 1 cup feta cheese, sliced

Directions:

1. Cut the tomatoes in half and then season them with salt, black pepper, and olive oil.
2. Press the sage leaves in the center of the tomatoes.
3. First, insert the grill grate in the ninja food grill and select the grill function.
4. Set the time to MAX for 8 minutes, buy selecting grill function.
5. Select start to begin preheating.
6. Once prehearing is done, arrange the tomato inside the unit onto grill grates.
7. Grill 4 to 6 minutes at MAX.
8. Remember to flip halfway through.
9. Once done, serve with feta cheese slices.

Nutrition:

- Calories: 345
- Fat: 23.5 g
- Sodium: 885 mg
- Carbs: 22.2 g
- Fiber: 4.3 g
- Sugar: 17.8 g
- Protein: 15.2 g

132. Mustard Green Veggies

Preparation time: 5 to 10 minutes
Cooking time: 30 to 40 minutes
Serving: 7 to 8
Ingredients:
Vinaigrette:

- 2 tbsp. Dijon mustard - 1/2 cup red wine vinegar
- 2 tbsp. honey - 1 tsp. salt - 1/4 tsp. black pepper
- 1/2 cup avocado oil - 1/2 cup olive oil

Veggies:

- 4 zucchinis, halved
- 4 sweet onions, quartered
- 4 red peppers, seeded and halved
- 2 bunches of green onions, trimmed
- 4 yellow squashes, cut in half

Directions:

1. In a small bowl, put the vinegar, mustard, honey, pepper, and salt and mix. Add the oils and combine them to make a smooth mixture.
2. Take Ninja Foodi Grill, place it over your kitchen stage, and open the top cover.
3. Arrange the grill grate and close its lid.
4. Press "GRILL" and choose the "MED" grill function. Set the timer to 10 minutes and then press "START/STOP." Ninja Foodi will start pre-heating. Ninja Foodi is preheated and prepared to cook when it begins to beep. After you hear a signal, open the top. Arrange the onion quarters over the grill grate.
5. Close it cover and cook for 5 minutes. Now open the top cover, flip the onions.
6. Close it cover and cook for 5 more minutes.
7. Grill the other vegetables in the same manner with 7 minutes per side for the zucchini, peppers, and squash. And 1 minute per side for the green onions. Serve the grilled veggies with the vinaigrette on top.

Nutrition:

- Calories: 326 Fat: 4.5 g Sat fat: 0.5 g
- Trans fat: 0 g Carbs: 35.5 g
- Fiber: 2 g Sodium: 524 mg
- Protein: 8 g

133. Vegetable Pasta Delight

Preparation time: 5 to 10 minutes
Cooking time: 15 minutes
Serving: 2 to 3
Ingredients:

- 1 small zucchini, sliced
- 1 small pepper sweet yellow, halved
- 2/3 cups orzo pasta, cooked and drained
- 1/4 lb. fresh asparagus, trimmed
- 1 small portobello mushroom, stem removed
- 1/2 small red onion, halved

Salad dressing:

- 2 tbsp. balsamic vinegar - 1 1/2 tbsp. lemon juice
- 2 garlic cloves, minced - 1 tbsp. olive oil
- 1/2 tsp. lemon-pepper seasoning

Salad:

- 1/2 tbsp. minced parsley
- 1/2 tbsp. minced basil - 1/4 tsp. salt
- 1/2 cup grape tomatoes halved - 1/8 tsp. pepper
- 1/2 cup (2 oz.) feta cheese, crumbled

Directions:

1. In 2 separate bowls, combine all the salad and dressing ingredients. Take Ninja Foodi Grill, place it over your kitchen stage, and open the top cover. Arrange the grill grate and close its lid.
2. Press "GRILL" and choose the "MED" grill function. Set the timer to 10 minutes and then press "START/STOP." Ninja Foodi will start pre-heating. Ninja Foodi is preheated and prepared to cook when it begins to beep. After you hear a signal, open the top.
3. Arrange the mushrooms, pepper, and onion over the grill grate. Close it cover and cook for 5 minutes. Now open the top cover, flip the vegetables. Close it cover and cook for 5 more minutes. Grill the other vegetables in the same manner with 2 minutes per side for the zucchini and asparagus. Dice the grilled vegetables; add them to the salad bowl. Add the pasta and top with the dressing; toss and serve.

Nutrition:

- Calories: 234 Fat: 14 g Sat fat: 1 g
- Trans fat: 0 g Carbs: 38 g Fiber: 4 g
- Sodium: 369 mg Protein: 12 g

134. Creamy Corn Potatoes

Preparation time: 5 to 10 minutes
Cooking time: 30 to 40 minutes
Serving: 4
Ingredients:

- 1 1/2 lb. red potatoes, quartered and boiled
- 3 tbsp. olive oil
- 1 tbsp. cilantro, minced
- 2 sweet corn ears, without husks
- 1/4 tsp. cayenne pepper
- 2 poblano peppers
- 1/2 cup milk - 1 tsp. ground cumin
- 1 tbsp. lime juice
- 1 jalapeno pepper, seeded and minced
- 1/2 cup sour cream - 1 1/2 tsp. garlic salt

Directions:

1. Drain the potatoes and rub them with oil.
2. Take Ninja Foodi Grill, place it over your kitchen stage, and open the top cover.
3. Arrange the grill grate and close its lid.
4. Press "GRILL" and choose the "MED" grill function. Set the timer to 10 minutes and then press "START/STOP." Ninja Foodi will start pre-heating. Ninja Foodi is preheated and prepared to cook when it begins to beep. After you hear a signal, open the top.
5. Arrange the poblano peppers over the grill grate.
6. Close it cover and cook for 5 minutes. Now open the top cover, flip the peppers.
7. Close it cover and cook for 5 more minutes.
8. Grill the other vegetables in the same manner with 7 minutes per side for the potatoes and corn.
9. Whisk the remaining ingredients in another bowl.
10. Peel the grilled pepper and chop them. Divide corn ears into smaller pieces and cut the potatoes as Serve the grilled veggies with the vinaigrette on top.

Nutrition:

- Calories: 322 Fat: 4.5 g
- Sat fat: 1 g Trans fat: 0 g Carbs: 51.5 g
- Fiber: 3 g Sodium: 600 mg Protein: 5 g

135. Cheese Stuffed Zucchini

Preparation time: 5 to 10 minutes
Cooking time: 8 minutes
Serving: 2
Ingredients:

- 5 oz. Parmesan, shredded
- 1/2 tsp. chili flakes
- 1/4 tsp. dried basil
- 1 zucchini
- 1/2 tsp. tomato paste
- 1 tsp. olive oil

Directions:

1. Take the zucchini; cut it into halves. Scoop the flesh from them and spread with the tomato paste inside the hollowed halves.
2. Add the shredded cheese. Sprinkle with chili flakes, dried basil, and olive oil.
3. Take Ninja Foodi multi-cooker, arrange it over a cooking platform, and open the top lid.
4. In the pot, arrange a reversible rack and place the Crisping Basket over the rack.
5. In the basket, add the zucchini halves.
6. Seal the multi-cooker by locking it with the crisping lid; ensure to keep the pressure release valve locked/sealed.
7. Select the "AIR CRISP" mode and adjust the 375°F temperature level. Then, set the timer to 8 minutes and press "STOP/START;" it will start the cooking process by building up inside pressure.
8. Once the timer goes off, fast-release pressure by adjusting the pressure valve to the VENT.
9. After pressure gets released, open the pressure lid. Serve warm and enjoy!

Nutrition:

- Calories: 326 Fat: 21 g
- Sat fat: 0 g
- Trans fat: 0 g
- Carbs: 6.5 g
- Fiber: 1 g
- Sodium: 458 mg
- Protein: 12.5 g

136. Broccoli Crisp

Preparation time: 5 to 10 minutes
Cooking time: 15 minutes
Serving: 4
Ingredients:

- 1/2 tsp. red pepper flakes
- 1/4 cup toasted sliced almonds
- 1 large head of broccoli, cut into florets
- 2 tbsp. extra-virgin olive oil
- Black pepper (ground) and salt to taste
- 2 tbsp. grated Parmesan cheese
- Lemon wedges, for serving

Directions:

1. In a mixing bowl, add the broccoli and toss it with olive oil. Season with salt and black pepper. Add the red pepper flakes and almonds and toss to combine.
2. Take Ninja Foodi multi-cooker, arrange it over a cooking platform, and open the top lid.
3. In the pot, arrange a reversible rack and place the Crisping Basket over the rack.
4. In the basket, add the broccoli mixture.
5. Seal the multi-cooker by locking it with the crisping lid; ensure to keep the pressure release valve locked/sealed.
6. Select the "AIR CRISP" mode and adjust the 390°F temperature level. Then, set the timer to 15 minutes and press "STOP/START"; it will start the cooking process by building up inside pressure.
7. Once the timer goes off, fast-release pressure by adjusting the pressure valve to the VENT.
8. After pressure gets released, open the pressure lid. Mix in the almonds.
9. Serve warm with the cheese on top and lemon wedges and enjoy!

Nutrition:

- Calories: 181 Fat: 11.5 g
- Sat fat: 3 g Trans fat: 0 g
- Carbs: 9 g Fiber: 4 g Sodium: 421 mg
- Protein: 7.5 g

137. Mashed Asparagus

Preparation time: 5 to 10 minutes
Cooking time: 10 minutes
Serving: 2
Ingredients:

- 1 tbsp. butter
- 1 tsp. cayenne pepper
- 1/2 tsp. chili pepper
- 3 cups vegetable broth
- 16 oz. asparagus, chopped
- 1/2 to 1/3 cup sour cream
- 1 tsp. paprika
- 1 tbsp. sriracha
- 2 tsp. salt

Directions:

1. Take Ninja Foodi multi-cooker, arrange it over a cooking platform, and open the top lid.
2. In the pot, add the chopped asparagus, cayenne pepper, salt, and broth
3. Seal the multi-cooker by locking it with the pressure lid; ensure to keep the pressure release valve locked/sealed.
4. Select "PRESSURE" mode and select the "HI" pressure level. Then, set the timer to 10 minutes and press "STOP/START;" it will start the cooking process by building up inside pressure.
5. Once the timer goes off, fast-release pressure by adjusting the pressure valve to the VENT. After pressure gets released, open the pressure lid.
6. Add the asparagus to a food processor or blender. Add the chile pepper, butter, sriracha, and sour cream. Blend the mixture until it becomes smooth.
7. Serve warm and enjoy!

Nutrition:

- Calories: 86 Fat: 8.5 g
- Sat fat: 1 g Trans fat: 0 g
- Carbs: 5 g Fiber: 1.5 g
- Sodium: 386 mg
- Protein: 4 g

138. Apple Green Salad

Preparation time: 5 to 10 minutes
Cooking time: 6 minutes
Serving: 2 to 3
Ingredients:

- 1/4 tsp. Sriracha chili sauce
- 2 tbsp. cilantro, chopped
- 1/4 cup blue cheese, crumbled
- 1 apple, wedged
- 2 tbsp. orange juice
- 3 tbsp. avocado oil
- 1 tbsp. honey
- 1/4 tsp. salt
- 2 tbsp. vinegar
- 1/2 garlic clove, minced
- 5 oz. salad greens

Directions:

1. In a mixing bowl, put the chili sauce, orange juice, oil, honey, vinegar, cilantro, garlic, and salt and mix. Add 1/4th on the dressing with the apples in another bowl; toss well.
2. Take Ninja Foodi Grill, place it over your kitchen stage, and open the top cover.
3. Arrange the grill grate and close its lid.
4. Press "GRILL" and choose the "MED" grill function. Set the timer to 6 minutes and then press "START/STOP." Ninja Foodi will start pre-heating.
5. Ninja Foodi is preheated and prepared to cook when it begins to beep. After you hear a signal, open the top. Arrange the apples over the grill grate. Close it cover and cook for 3 minutes. Now open the top cover, flip the apples.
6. Close it cover and cook for 3 more minutes.
7. Combine other ingredients in another bowl. Add the apples and top with the remaining dressing.
8. Serve warm.

Nutrition:

- Calories: 406 Fat: 5 g Sat fat: 1.5 g
- Trans fat: 0 g Carbs: 48 g Fiber: 3 g
- Sodium: 517 mg Protein: 2 g

139. Spinach Olive Meal

Preparation time: 5 to 10 minutes
Cooking time: 15 minutes
Serving: 5 to 6
Ingredients:

- 2/3 cup Kalamata olives, halved and pitted
- 1 1/2 cups feta cheese, grated
- 4 tbsp. butter
- 2 lb. spinach, chopped and boiled
- Ground black pepper and salt to taste
- 4 tsp. grated lemon zest

Directions:

1. In a mixing bowl, add the spinach, butter, salt, pepper.
2. Take Ninja Foodi multi-cooker, arrange it over a cooking platform, and open the top lid.
3. In the pot, arrange a reversible rack and place the Crisping Basket over the rack.
4. In the basket, add the spinach mixture.
5. Seal the multi-cooker by locking it with the crisping lid; ensure to keep the pressure release valve locked/sealed.
6. Select the "AIR CRISP" mode and adjust the 340°F temperature level. Then, set the timer to 15 minutes and press "STOP/START;" it will start the cooking process by building up inside pressure.
7. Once the timer goes off, fast-release pressure by adjusting the pressure valve to the VENT.
8. After pressure gets released, open the pressure lid. Add olives, cheese, and lemon zest.
9. Serve warm and enjoy!

Nutrition:

- Calories: 253
- Fat: 18 g
- Sat fat: 3 g
- Trans fat: 0 g
- Carbs: 8 g
- Fiber: 4 g
- Sodium: 339 mg
- Protein: 10.5 g

140. Spinach Chickpea Stew

Preparation time: 5 to 10 minutes
Cooking time: 5 minutes
Serving: 5 to 6
Ingredients:

- 4 sweet potatoes, peeled and diced
- 4 cups vegetable broth
- 1 tbsp. extra-virgin olive oil
- 1 yellow onion, diced - 4 garlic cloves, minced
- 4 cups baby spinach - 2 (15 oz.) cans chickpeas, drained - 1 (15 oz.) can fire-roasted diced tomatoes, undrained - 1 tsp. ground coriander
- 1/2 tsp. black pepper, freshly ground
- 1/2 tsp. paprika - 1/2 tsp. sea salt
- 1 1/2 tsp. ground cumin

Directions:

1. Take Ninja Foodi multi-cooker, arrange it over a cooking platform, and open the top lid.
2. In the pot, add the oil; Select "SEAR/SAUTÉ" mode and select "MD: HI" pressure level.
3. Press "STOP/START." After about 4 to 5 minutes, the oil will start simmering.
4. Add the onions, garlic, and cook (while stirring) until they become softened and translucent. Add the sweet potatoes, broth, tomatoes, chickpeas, cumin, coriander, paprika, salt, and black pepper; stir the mixture.
5. Seal the multi-cooker by locking it with the pressure lid; ensure to keep the pressure release valve locked/sealed. Select "PRESSURE" mode and select the "HI" pressure level. Then, set the timer to 8 minutes and press "STOP/START;" it will start the cooking process by building up inside pressure. Once the timer goes off, fast-release pressure by adjusting the pressure valve to the VENT. After pressure gets released, open the pressure lid. Select "SEAR/SAUTÉ" mode and select the "MD" pressure level; add the spinach and combine. Stir-cook until wilts.
6. Serve warm and enjoy!

Nutrition:

- Calories: 234 Fat: 4.5 g
- Sat fat: 0 g Trans fat: 0 g Carbs: 39.5 g
- Fiber: 9 g Sodium: 576 mg Protein: 8 g

141. Stuffed Tomatoes

Preparation time: 15 minutes
Cooking time: 14 minutes
Serving: 2
Ingredients:

- 2 large tomatoes
- 1/2 cup broccoli, chopped finely
- 1/2 cup cheddar cheese, shredded
- 1 tbsp. unsalted butter, melted
- 1/2 tsp. dried thyme, crushed

Directions:

1. Carefully cut the top of each tomato and scoop out pulp and seeds.
2. In a bowl, place the chopped broccoli and cheese and mix.
3. Stuff each tomato with broccoli mixture evenly.
4. Arrange the "Crisper Basket" in the pot of Ninja Foodi Grill.
5. Close the Ninja Foodi Grill with lid and select "Air Crisp."
6. Set the temperature to 355°F to preheat.
7. Press "Start/Stop" to begin preheating.
8. When the display shows "Add Food" open the lid and place the tomatoes into the "Crisper Basket".
9. Drizzle the tomatoes with butter.
10. Close the Ninja Foodi Grill with a lid and set the time for 15 minutes.
11. Press "Start/Stop" to begin cooking.
12. When cooking time is completed, press "Start/Stop" to stop cooking and open the lid.
13. Serve with the garnishing of thyme.

Nutrition:

- Calories: 206
- Fat: 15.6 g
- Sat fat: 9.7 g
- Carbs: 9.1 g
- Fiber: 2.9 g
- Sugar: 5.3 g
- Protein: 9.4 g

142. Herbed Mushrooms

Preparation time: 15 minutes
Cooking time: 8 minutes
Serving: 2
Ingredients:

- 8 oz. button mushrooms, stemmed
- 2 tbsp. olive oil
- 2 tbsp. Italian dried mixed herbs
- Salt and freshly ground black pepper, to taste
- 1 tsp. dried dill

Directions:

1. Wash and trim thin slices from the ends of the stems.
2. In a bowl, mix together the mushrooms, dried herbs, oil, salt, and black pepper.
3. Arrange the greased "Crisper Basket" in the pot of Ninja Foodi Grill.
4. Close the Ninja Foodi Grill with lid and select "Air Crisp".
5. Set the temperature to 355°F to preheat.
6. Press "Start/Stop" to begin preheating.
7. When the display shows "Add Food" open the lid and place the mushrooms' hollow part upwards into the "Crisper Basket".
8. Close the Ninja Foodi Grill with a lid and set the time for 8 minutes.
9. Press "Start/Stop" to begin cooking.
10. When cooking time is completed, press "Start/Stop" to stop cooking and open the lid.
11. Serve with the garnishing of dill.

Nutrition:

- Calories: 149
- Fat: 14.4 g
- Sat fat: 2 g
- Carbs: 4.7 g
- Fiber: 1.7 g
- Sugar: 2 g
- Protein: 3.8 g

143. Glazed Carrots

Preparation time: 10 minutes
Cooking time: 12 minutes
Serving: 4
Ingredients:

- 3 cups carrots, peeled and cut into large chunks
- 1 tbsp. olive oil
- 1 tbsp. honey
- 1 tbsp. fresh thyme, finely chopped
- Salt and freshly ground black pepper, to taste

Directions:

1. In a bowl, add the carrot, oil, honey, thyme, salt, and black pepper and mix until well combined.
2. Arrange the "Crisper Basket" in the pot of Ninja Foodi Grill.
3. Close the Ninja Foodi Grill with lid and select "Air Crisp".
4. Set the temperature to 390°F to preheat.
5. Press "Start/Stop" to begin preheating.
6. When the display shows "Add Food" open the lid and place the carrot chunks into the "Crisper Basket" in a single layer.
7. Close the Ninja Foodi Grill with a lid and set the time for 12 minutes.
8. Press "Start/Stop" to begin cooking.
9. When the cooking time is completed, press "Start/Stop" to stop cooking and open the lid.
10. Serve hot.

Nutrition:

- Calories: 82
- Fat: 3.6 g
- Sat fat: 0.5 g
- Carbs: 12.9 g
- Fiber: 0.3 g
- Sugar: 8.4 g
- Protein: 0.8 g

144. Lemony Green Beans

Preparation time: 10 minutes
Cooking time: 12 minutes
Serving: 4
Ingredients:

- 1 lb. fresh green beans, trimmed
- 1 tbsp. butter, melted
- 1 tbsp. fresh lemon juice
- 1/4 tsp. garlic powder
- Salt and freshly ground black pepper, to taste
- 1/2 tsp. lemon zest, grated

Directions:

1. In a large bowl, add all the ingredients except the lemon zest and toss to coat well.
2. Arrange the "Crisper Basket" in the pot of Ninja Foodi Grill.
3. Close the Ninja Foodi Grill with lid and select "Air Crisp".
4. Set the temperature to 400°F to preheat.
5. Press "Start/Stop" to begin preheating.
6. When the display shows "Add Food" open the lid and place the green beans into the "Crisper Basket."
7. Close the Ninja Foodi Grill with a lid and set the time for 12 minutes.
8. Press "Start/Stop" to begin cooking.
9. When the cooking time is completed, press "Start/Stop" to stop cooking and open the lid.
10. Serve warm with the garnishing of lemon zest.

Nutrition:

- Calories: 62
- Fat: 3.1 g
- Sat fat: 1.9 g
- Carbs: 8.4 g
- Fiber: 3.9 g
- Sugar: 1.7 g
- Protein: 2.2 g

145. Vinegar Brussels Sprout

Preparation time: 10 minutes
Cooking time: 20 minutes
Serving: 4
Ingredients:

- 1 lb. Brussels sprouts, ends trimmed and cut into bite-sized pieces
- 1 tbsp. balsamic vinegar
- 1 tbsp. olive oil
- Salt and freshly ground black pepper, to taste

Directions:

1. In a bowl, add all the ingredients and toss to coat well.
2. Arrange the "Crisper Basket" in the pot of Ninja Foodi Grill.
3. Close the Ninja Foodi Grill with lid and select "Air Crisp".
4. Set the temperature to 350°F to preheat.
5. Press "Start/Stop" to begin preheating.
6. When the display shows "Add Food" open the lid and place the Brussels sprouts into the "Crisper Basket."
7. Close the Ninja Foodi Grill with a lid and set the time for 20 minutes.
8. Press "Start/Stop" to begin cooking.
9. When the cooking time is completed, press "Start/Stop" to stop cooking and open the lid.
10. Serve hot.

Nutrition:

- Calories: 80
- Fat: 3.9 g
- Sat fat: 0.6 g
- Carbs: 10.3 g
- Fiber: 4.3 g
- Sugar: 2.5 g
- Protein: 3.9 g

146. Nutty Acorn Squash

Preparation time: 10 minutes
Cooking time: 25 minutes
Serving: 2
Ingredients:

- 1 medium acorn squash
- 2 tsp. olive oil
- 2 tbsp. pecans, chopped
- 1 tbsp. brown sugar
- 1/2 tsp. ground cinnamon
- 1/8 tsp. ground cloves

Directions:

1. Cut the acorn squash in half lengthwise.
2. Brush the flesh side of each squash half with oil.
3. In a bowl, add the remaining ingredients and mix.
4. Arrange the "Crisper Basket" in the pot of Ninja Foodi Grill.
5. Close the Ninja Foodi Grill with lid and select "Air Crisp".
6. Set the temperature to 375°F to preheat.
7. Press "Start/Stop" to begin preheating.
8. When the display shows "Add Food" open the lid and place the squash halves, cut side up into the "Crisper Basket".
9. Close the Ninja Foodi Grill with a lid and set the time for 25 minutes.
10. Press "Start/Stop" to begin cooking.
11. When the cooking time is completed, press "Start/Stop" to stop cooking and open the lid.
12. Serve warm.

Nutrition:

- Calories: 254
- Fat: 11.1 g
- Sat fat: 1.4 g
- Carbs: 41.6 g
- Fiber: 6.4 g
- Sugar: 4.7 g
- Protein: 3.7 g

147. Stuffed Potatoes

Preparation time: 15 minutes
Cooking time: 26 minutes
Serving: 4
Ingredients:

- 4 potatoes, peeled - 2 to 3 tbsp. canola oil
- 1 tbsp. butter - 1/2 of brown onion, chopped
- 2 tbsp. fresh chives, chopped
- 1/2 cup Parmesan cheese, grated

Directions:

1. Coat the potatoes with some oil.
2. Arrange the "Crisper Basket" in the pot of Ninja Foodi Grill. Close the Ninja Foodi Grill with lid and select "Air Crisp". Set the temperature to 390°F to preheat. Press "Start/Stop" to begin preheating. When the display shows "Add Food" open the lid and place the potatoes into the "Crisper Basket."Close the Ninja Foodi Grill with a lid and set the time for 20 minutes.
3. Press "Start/Stop" to begin cooking.
4. Coat the potatoes twice with the remaining oil.
5. Meanwhile, in a frying pan, melt the butter over medium heat and sauté the onion for about 4 to 5 minutes. Remove from the heat and transfer the onion into a bowl. In the bowl of onion, add the potato flesh, chives, and half of the cheese and stir to combine. When cooking time is completed, press "Start/Stop" to stop cooking and open the lid.Transfer the potatoes onto a platter. Carefully cut each potato in half.
6. With a small scooper, scoop out the flesh from each half. Stuff the potato halves with the potato mixture evenly and sprinkle with the remaining cheese. Again, arrange the potato halves in the "Crisper Basket." Close the Ninja Foodi Grill with lid and select "Air Crisp. Set the temperature to 390°F for 6 minutes. Press "Start/Stop" to begin cooking. When cooking time is completed, press "Start/Stop" to stop cooking and open the lid. Serve immediately.

Nutrition:

- Calories: 276 Fat: 12.5 g Sat fat: 3.6 g
- Carbs: 34.8 g Fiber: 5.4 g Sugar: 3.1 g
- Protein: 7.8 g

148. Vegetarian Stuffed Bell Peppers

Preparation time: 15 minutes
Cooking time: 15 minutes
Serving: 5
Ingredients:

- 1/2 of small bell pepper, seeded and chopped
- 1 (15 oz.) can diced tomatoes with juice
- 1 (15 oz.) can red kidney beans, rinsed and drained
- 1 cup cooked rice
- 1 1/2 tsp. Italian seasoning
- 5 large bell peppers, tops removed and seeded
- 1/2 cup mozzarella cheese, shredded
- 1 tbsp. Parmesan cheese, grated

Directions:

1. In a bowl, mix together the chopped bell pepper, tomatoes with juice, beans, rice, and Italian seasoning. Stuff each bell pepper with the rice mixture.
2. Arrange the greased "Crisper Basket" in the pot of Ninja Foodi Grill.
3. Close the Ninja Foodi Grill with lid and select "Air Crisp."Set the temperature to 360°F to preheat. Press "Start/Stop" to begin preheating.
4. When the display shows "Add Food" open the lid and place the bell peppers into the "Crisper Basket. Close the Ninja Foodi Grill with a lid and set the time for 15 minutes.
5. Press "Start/Stop" to begin cooking.
6. Meanwhile, in a bowl, mix together the mozzarella and Parmesan cheese.
7. After 12 minutes of cooking, top each bell pepper with a cheese mixture.
8. When cooking time is completed, press "Start/Stop" to stop cooking and open the lid.
9. Transfer the bell peppers onto a serving platter and serve warm.

Nutrition:

- Calories: 282 Fat: 2.8 g Sat fat: 1.1 g
- Carbs: 54.9 g Fiber: 9.2 g Sugar: 8.3 g
- Protein: 11.4 g

149. Green Beans Casserole

Preparation time: 15 minutes
Cooking time: 32 minutes
Serving: 6
Ingredients:

- 1 1/2 lb. fresh green beans, trimmed
- 2 cups fresh mushrooms, chopped
- 1 cup onion, chopped
- 1 tbsp. all-purpose flour
- 1 (14 oz.) can full-fat coconut milk
- 3/4 cup vegetable broth
- Olive oil to taste

Directions:

1. In a pan of boiling water, add the green beans and cook for about 5 to 7 minutes.
2. Drain the green beans and rinse in cold water.
3. Drain again and set aside.
4. In a skillet, heat the oil over medium heat and sauté the mushrooms and onions for about 5 to 6 minutes.
5. Add the flour and stir to combine.
6. Stir in the coconut milk and broth and remove from the heat.
7. In the bottom of a greased baking pan, place the cooked green beans and top with broth mixture.
8. Arrange the "Crisper Basket" in the pot of Ninja Foodi Grill. Close the Ninja Foodi Grill with lid and select "Air Crisp."
9. Set the temperature to 370°F to preheat.
10. Press "Start/Stop" to begin preheating.
11. When the display shows "Add Food" open the lid and place the pan into the "Crisper Basket."
12. Close the Ninja Foodi Grill with a lid and set the time for 15 minutes. Press "Start/Stop" to begin cooking. When cooking time is completed, press "Start/Stop" to stop cooking and open the lid.
13. Serve warm.

Nutrition:

- Calories: 179 Fat: 12.6 g
- Sat fat: 11.3 g Carbs: 13.8 g Fiber: 4.5 g
- Sugar: 3.9 g Protein: 4.8 g

150. Tofu With Orange Sauce

Preparation time: 15 minutes
Cooking time: 20 minutes
Serving: 4
Ingredients:
For tofu:

- 1 lb. extra-firm tofu pressed and cubed
- 1 tbsp. cornstarch
- 1 tbsp. tamari

For sauce:

- 1/2 cup water
- 1/3 cup fresh orange juice
- 1 tbsp. honey
- 1 tsp. orange zest, grated
- 1 tsp. garlic, minced
- 1 tsp. fresh ginger, minced
- 2 tsp. cornstarch
- 1/4 tsp. red pepper flakes, crushed

Directions:

1. In a bowl, add the tofu, cornstarch, and tamari and toss to coat well.
2. Set the tofu aside to marinate for at least 15 minutes.
3. Arrange the greased "Crisper Basket" in the pot of Ninja Foodi Grill.
4. Close the Ninja Foodi Grill with lid and select "Air Crisp."
5. Set the temperature to 390°F to preheat.
6. Press "Start/Stop" to begin preheating.
7. When the display shows "Add Food" open the lid and place the tofu cubes into the "Crisper Ninja Foodi Grill with lid and set the time for 10 minutes.
8. Press "Start/Stop" to begin cooking.
9. Meanwhile, for the sauce: in a small pan, add all the ingredients over medium-high heat and bring to a boil, stirring continuously.
10. When the cooking time is completed, press "Start/Stop" to stop cooking.
11. Open the lid and transfer the tofu into a serving bowl.
12. Add the sauce and gently stir to combine.
13. Serve immediately.

Nutrition:

- Calories: 147
- Fat: 6.7 g
- Sat fat: 0.6 g
- Carbs: 12.7 g
- Fiber: 0.7 g
- Sugar: 6.7 g
- Protein: 12.1 g

CHAPTER 8:

Fish And Seafood

151. Perfect Spanish Garlic Shrimp

Preparation time: 5 to 10 minutes
Cooking time: 10 minutes
Serving: 3
Ingredients:

- 1 lemon, cut into wedges
- 1/2 tsp. red pepper flakes
- 1/2 tsp. salt
- 1/2 cup olive oil
- 1 and 1/2 lb. shrimp, shelled and deveined
- 2 garlic cloves, minced

Directions:

1. Rinse the shrimp and pat dry with paper towels. Combine the shrimp, olive oil, garlic, salt, and red pepper flakes in a medium bowl.
2. Toss gently to combine. Cover with plastic wrap and then refrigerate for at least 30 minutes or up to 2 hours.
3. Insert the Grill Grate and close the hood.
4. Select GRILL, set temperature to HIGH, and set time to 8 minutes. Select START/STOP to begin pre-heating.
5. Grill the shrimp for about 3 minutes, until they are opaque and firm to the touch. Serve the shrimp immediately in 4 small bowls with lemon wedges.

Nutrition:

- Calories: 453
- Fat: 42 g
- Sat fat: 15 g
- Carbs: 4 g
- Fiber: 2 g
- Sodium: 644 mg
- Protein: 16 g

152. Curried Shrimp and Potato Kebabs

Preparation time: 30 minutes
Cooking time: 30 minutes
Serving: 4
Ingredients:

- 12 new or baby potatoes
- 3 garlic cloves, minced
- 1/4 tsp. salt
- 3 tbsp. canola oil
- 2 tbsp. chopped fresh cilantro
- 1 tbsp. curry powder
- 20 peeled and deveined raw shrimp, tails left on (20 to 25 per lb.; see Tip)
- 1/2 cup nonfat plain yogurt
- 1 tsp. lime juice

Directions:

1. Preheat the grill for eight minutes.
2. Put potatoes in a container. Microwave on High until they get tender when pierced with a fork, three to three and a half minutes.
3. Meanwhile, mix oil, cilantro, garlic, curry powder, and salt in a big bowl. Reserve 2 tbsp. the mixture in a bowl. Add shrimp and potatoes to a large bowl; toss it to coat. Thread the shrimp and potatoes onto 4 twelve-inch skewers.
4. Insert grill grate in the unit and close the hood. Select the option GRILL, set the temperature to LOW, and set the time to five minutes. Select the option START/STOP to begin preheating.
5. Stir the yogurt and lime juice in a small bowl of the reserved sauce. Serve each kebab with 2 tbsp. sauce.

Nutrition:

- Calories: 244
- Fat: 12 g
- Carbs: 15 g
- Protein: 19 g

153. Shrimp Po'Boy

Preparation time: 30 minutes
Cooking time: 30 minutes
Serving: 4
Ingredients:

- 2 cups finely shredded red cabbage
- 2 tbsp. dill pickle relish
- 1 lb. peeled and deveined raw shrimp, (51 to 60 per lb.; see Shopping Tip)
- 4 tsp. canola oil, divided
- 2 tbsp. reduced-fat mayonnaise
- 2 tbsp. nonfat plain yogurt
- 1 tsp. chili powder
- 1/2 tsp. paprika
- 4 tomato slices, halved
- 1/4 cup thinly sliced red onion
- 1/4 tsp. freshly ground pepper
- 4 whole-wheat hot dog buns, or small sub rolls, split

Directions:

1. Preheat the grill for 8 minutes.
2. Combine the cabbage, mayonnaise relish, and yogurt in a medium bowl.
3. Toss the shrimp with 2 tsp. oil, paprika, chili powder, pickle relish, and pepper in a medium bowl. Place the remaining two tsp. oil in a bowl. Dip it in a pastry brush in the water, then in the oil, and then brush the insides of each bun.
4. Insert grill grate in the unit and close the hood. Select the option GRILL, set the temperature to LOW, and set the time to five minutes. Select the option START/STOP to begin preheating.
5. For assembling the sandwiches, divide the tomato and onion among the buns. Spread about one-third cup of cabbage mixture down the middle of each and top with about 1/2 cup grilled shrimp.

Nutrition:

- Calories: 285 Fat: 9 g
- Carbs: 30 g Protein: 21 g

154. Grilled Shrimp Cocktail With Yellow Gazpacho Salsa

Preparation time: 40 minutes
Cooking time: 60 minutes
Serving: 4
Ingredients:

- 4 medium yellow tomatoes, (1 lb.), seeded and finely chopped
- 1 stalk celery, finely chopped
- 1/2 small red onion, finely chopped
- 1 yellow bell pepper, finely chopped
- 1 medium cucumber, peeled, seeded, and finely chopped
- 1 tbsp. Worcestershire sauce
- 1/2 tsp. freshly ground pepper
- 2 tbsp. minced fresh chives
- 2 tbsp. white-wine vinegar
- 2 tbsp. lemon juice - 1/4 tsp. salt
- Several dashes of hot sauce, to taste
- 1 lb. raw shrimp, (21 to 25 per lb.; see Note), peeled and deveined
- 2 garlic cloves, minced
- 2 tbsp. minced fresh thyme

Directions:

1. Preheat the grill for 8 minutes.
2. Mix the tomatoes, cucumber, celery, bell pepper, onion, vinegar, lemon juice, chives, Worcestershire sauce, salt and pepper, and hot sauce in a big bowl. Cover it and chill for at least 20 minutes or for a single day.
3. Mix the shrimp, garlic, and thyme in a medium bowl; cover it and refrigerate for 20 minutes.
4. Insert grill grates in the unit and close the hood. Select the option GRILL, set the temperature to LOW, and set time to 2 minutes per side. Select the option START/STOP to begin preheating. Serve the shrimp with salsa in martini glasses.

Nutrition:

- Calories: 154 Fat: 2 g
- Carbs: 12 g Protein: 22 g

155. Grilled Salmon Packets

Preparation time: 5 minutes
Cooking time: 15 to 20 minutes
Serving: 4
Ingredients:

- 4 salmon steaks (6 oz. each)
- 1 tsp. lemon-pepper seasoning
- 1 cup shredded carrots
- 1 tsp. dried parsley flakes
- 1/2 cup julienned sweet yellow pepper
- 1/2 cup julienned green pepper
- 4 tsp. lemon juice
- 1/2 tsp. salt
- 1/4 tsp. pepper

Directions:

1. Preheat the grill for 5 minutes.
2. Sprinkle the salmon with lemon pepper. Place each of the salmon steaks on a double thickness of heavy-duty foil (about 12 in. square). Top with carrots and peppers. Sprinkle with remaining ingredients.
3. Fold foil around fish and seal them tightly. Then Grill, covered, over medium heat for 15 to 20 minutes or until fish flakes easily with a fork.

Nutrition:

- Calories: 280
- Fat: 16 g
- Carbs: 5 g
- Protein: 29 g

156. Grilled Lemon-Garlic Salmon

Preparation time: 10 minutes
Cooking time: 15 to 20 minutes
Serving: 4
Ingredients:

- 2 garlic cloves, minced
- 1/2 tsp. minced fresh rosemary
- 2 tsp. grated lemon zest
- 1/2 tsp. salt
- 1/2 tsp. pepper
- 4 salmon fillets (6 oz. each)

Directions:

1. Take a small bowl, mix the first 5 ingredients, and rub over fillets. Let it stand for 15 minutes. Coat the grill with cooking oil.
2. Preheat the grill for 8 minutes before use. Place salmon on the grill with the skin side up. Grill while covered over medium heat or broil 4 in. From heat 4 minutes. Turn and grill 3 to 6 minutes longer or until fish just begins to flake easily with a fork.

Nutrition:

- Calories: 264
- Fat: 16 g
- Carbs: 1 g
- Protein: 29 g

157. Apricot-Chile Glazed Salmon

Preparation time: 25 minutes
Cooking time: 25 minutes
Serving: 4
Ingredients:

- 2 tbsp. New Mexico red chili powder
- 3 tbsp. apricot jam
- 1/2 tsp. salt
- 1 1/4 to 1 1/2 lb. center-cut wild salmon (see Tip), skinned

Directions:

1. Preheat the grill for 8 minutes.
2. Combine the salt and chili powder in a bowl. Rub them onto both sides of the salmon.
3. Place the jam in a saucepan; heat it over medium heat, keep stirring it until melted.
4. Insert grill grate in the unit and close the hood.
5. Select the option GRILL, set the temperature to MED, and set the time to 10 minutes. Select the option START/STOP to begin preheating. Use a pastry brush, coat the top of the salmon with the jam. Close the grill; cook until the salmon easily flakes with a fork, 3 to 5 minutes more. To serve, cut into 4 portions.

Nutrition:

- Calories: 218
- Fat: 6 g
- Carbs: 12 g
- Protein: 29 g

158. Grilled Salmon With Mustard and Herbs

Preparation time: 15 minutes
Cooking time: 40 minutes
Serving: 4
Ingredients:

- 2 lemons, thinly sliced, plus 1 lemon cut into wedges for garnish
- 20 to 30 sprigs mixed fresh herbs, plus 2 tbsp. chopped, divided
- 1 tbsp. Dijon mustard
- 1 lb. center-cut salmon, skinned
- 1 garlic clove
- 1/4 tsp. salt

Directions:

1. Preheat the grill for 8 minutes.
2. Lay the 2 (9-inch) pieces of heavy-duty foil on top of one another and place them on a baking sheet. Arrange the lemon slices in 2 layers in the center of the foil. Spread the herb sprigs on the lemons. With the chef's knife, mash the garlic with salt and form a paste. Transfer it to a small dish and then stir in mustard and the remaining 2 tbsp. chopped herbs. Spread the mixture on double sides of the salmon. Place the salmon on top of the herb sprigs.
3. Slide off the foil and salmon from the baking sheet onto the grill Insert grill grate in the unit and close the hood. Select the option GRILL, set the temperature to MAX, and set the time to twenty-four minutes. Select the option START/STOP to begin preheating.
4. Divide the salmon into 4 portions and serve it with lemon wedges.

Nutrition:

- Calories: 132
- Fat: 4 g
- Carbs: 1 g
- Protein: 23 g

159. Grilled Salmon Soft Tacos

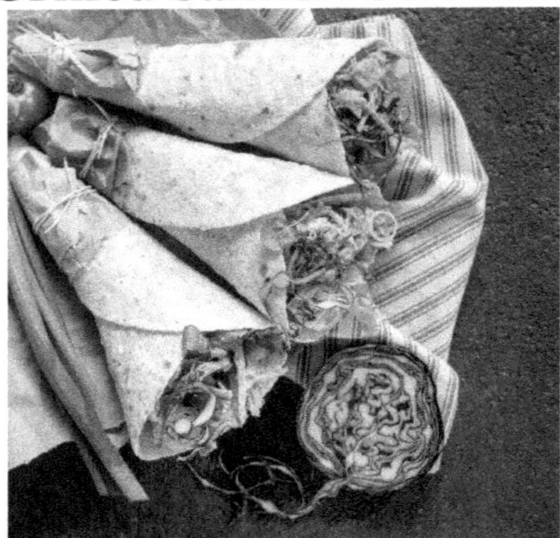

Preparation time: 20 minutes
Cooking time: 20 minutes
Serving: 4
Ingredients:

- 2 tbsp. extra-virgin olive oil
- 1 tbsp. ancho or New Mexico chile powder
- 4 (4 oz.) wild salmon fillets, about 1-inch thick, skin on
- 1 tbsp. fresh lime juice
- 1/4 tsp. kosher salt
- 1/8 tsp. freshly ground pepper
- 8 (6-inch) corn or flour tortillas, warmed
- Cabbage Slaw, (recipe follows) to taste
- Citrus Salsa, (recipe follows) to taste
- Cilantro Crema, (recipe follows) to taste

Directions:

1. Preheat the grill for 8 minutes.
2. Combine chili powder, oil, lime juice, salt, and pepper in a bowl. Rub the spice mixture over salmon. Insert grill grate in the unit and close the hood. Select the option GRILL, set the temperature to LOW, and set the time to 8 minutes. Select the option START/STOP to begin preheating. Cut each of the fillets lengthwise into 2 pieces and then remove the skin.
3. To serve, place 2 tortillas on each plate. Divide the fish, Citrus Salsa, Cabbage Slaw, and Cilantro Crema among the tortillas.

Nutrition:

- Calories: 570
- Fat: 30 g
- Carbs: 44 g
- Protein: 31 g

160. Easy BBQ Roast Shrimp

Preparation time: 5 to 10 minutes
Cooking time: 7 minutes
Serving: 2
Ingredients:

- 1/2 lb. shrimps, large
- 3 tbsp. chipotle in adobo sauce, minced
- 1/2 orange, juiced
- 1/4 cup BBQ sauce
- 1/4 tsp. salt

Directions:

1. Add listed ingredients into a mixing bowl
2. Mix them well
3. Keep it aside
4. Pre-heat Ninja Foodi by pressing the "ROAST" option and setting it to "400°F."
5. Set the timer to 7 minutes
6. Let it pre-heat until you hear a beep
7. Arrange shrimps over Grill Grate and lock lid
8. cook for 7 minutes
9. Serve and enjoy!

Nutrition:

- Calories: 173
- Fat: 2 g
- Sat fat: 0.5 g
- Carbs: 21 g
- Fiber: 2 g
- Sodium: 1143 mg
- Protein: 17 g

161. Paprika Grilled Shrimp

Preparation time: 5 to 10 minutes
Cooking time: 6 minutes
Serving: 4
Ingredients:

- 1 lb. jumbo shrimps, peeled and deveined
- 2 tbsp. brown sugar
- 1 tbsp. paprika
- 1 tbsp. garlic powder
- 2 tbsp. olive oil
- 1 tsp. garlic salt
- 1/2 tsp. black pepper

Directions:

1. Add listed ingredients into a mixing bowl
2. Mix them well
3. Let it chill and marinate for 30 to 60 minutes
4. Pre-heat Ninja Foodi by pressing the "GRILL" option and setting it to "MED."
5. Set the timer to 6 minutes
6. Let it pre-heat until you hear a beep
7. Arrange prepared shrimps over the grill grate
8. Lock lid and cook for 3 minutes
9. Then flip and cook for 3 minutes more
10. Serve and enjoy!

Nutrition:

- Calories: 370
- Fat: 27 g
- Sat fat: 3 g
- Carbs: 23 g
- Fiber: 8 g
- Sodium: 182 mg
- Protein: 6 g

162. Grilled Salmon With White Bean and Arugula Salad

Preparation time: 15 minutes
Cooking time: 10 minutes
Serving: 4
Ingredients:

- 1/4 tsp. grated lemon rind
- 3 tbsp. fresh lemon juice
- 1 tbsp. chopped capers, rinsed and drained
- 2 tbsp. olive oil
- 1/8 tsp. ground red pepper
- 3/4 tsp. kosher salt, divided
- 1/2 tsp. minced fresh garlic
- 1 (15 oz.) can unsalted Great Northern beans, rinsed and drained
- 1/4 tsp. freshly ground black pepper
- Cooking spray
- 4 (6 oz.) salmon fillets
- 4 cups loosely packed arugula
- 1/2 cup thinly sliced red onion

Directions:

1. Mix together juice, oil, capers, rind, 1/2 tsp. salt, garlic, and red pepper in a bowl.
2. Place beans in the bowl and drizzle with 2 tbsp. caper mixture.
3. Heat a grill for 8 minutes before use. Coat the grill with cooking oil. Coat the salmon with cooking oil and sprinkle with the remaining 1/4 tsp. salt along with black pepper. Add salmon to grill while skin side down. Grill for 6 minutes. Turn salmon over; grill for 1 minute or until done. Keep them warm.
4. Add arugula along with onions to the bowl with beans. Sprinkle with the remaining caper mixture and toss. Divide salad among four plates; top each serving with one fillet. Serve immediately.

Nutrition:

- Calories: 379 Fat: 15 g
- Carbs: 21 g Protein: 40 g

163. Teriyaki-Marinated Salmon

Preparation time: 5 minutes
Cooking time: 8 minutes
Serving: 4
Ingredients:

- 4 uncooked skinless salmon fillets (6 oz. each)
- 1 cup teriyaki marinade

Directions:

1. Put the fish fillets and teriyaki sauce in a big resealable plastic bag. Move the fillets around to coat everywhere with sauce. Refrigerate it for 1 to 12 hours as per your need.
2. Insert the grill grate in the unit and close the hood. Select the option GRILL, set the temperature to MAX, and set the time to eight minutes. Press START/STOP to begin preheating.
3. When the unit signals that it has preheated, put fillets on the grill, gently press them to maximize the grill marks. Close the hood and cook it for 6 minutes. There isn't a need to flip the fish while cooking.
4. After 6 minutes, check the fillets if done; the internal temperature should come at least 140°F. If necessary, close the hood and continue to cook for 2 more minutes.
5. After cooking, serve the fillets immediately.

Nutrition:

- Calories: 261
- Fat: 10.6 g
- Carbs: 8 g
- Protein: 33.3 g
-

164. Grilled Fish Tacos

Preparation time: 30 minutes
Cooking time: 50 minutes
Serving: 6
Ingredients:

- 4 tsp. chili powder, preferably made with New Mexico or ancho chiles (see Note)
- 2 tbsp. lime juice - 2 tbsp. extra-virgin olive oil
- 1 tsp. ground cumin - 1 tsp. onion powder
- 1 tsp. garlic powder - 1 tsp. salt
- 1/2 tsp. freshly ground pepper
- 2 lb. mahi-mahi or Pacific halibut (see Note), 1/2- 3/4 inch thick, skinned, and cut into 4 portions - 1/4 cup reduced-fat sour cream
- 1/4 cup low-fat mayonnaise
- 2 tbsp. chopped fresh cilantro - 1 tsp. lime zest
- Freshly ground pepper to taste
- 3 cups finely shredded red or green cabbage
- 2 tbsp. lime juice - 1 tsp. sugar - 1/8 tsp. salt
- 12 corn tortillas, warmed

Directions:

1. To prepare the fish: Combine lime juice, chili powder, oil, cumin, onion powder, salt and pepper, garlic powder in a bowl. Rub the adobo over all the fish. Let it stand 20 to 30 minutes for the fish to absorb the flavor.
2. To prepare the coleslaw: Add lime juice, sour cream, mayonnaise, cilantro, lime zest, salt and pepper, sugar, in a medium bowl; mix them until smooth and creamy. Add the cabbage and toss it to combine. Refrigerate until ready to use.
3. Preheat the grill for 8 minutes before use.
4. Insert grill grate in the unit and close the hood. Select the option GRILL, set the temperature to LOW, and set the time to fifteen minutes. Select the option START/STOP to begin preheating.
5. Transfer the fish to a plate and then separate it into large chunks. Serve the tacos by passing the fish, tortillas, coleslaw, and taco garnishes separately

Nutrition:

- Calories: 334 Fat: 10 g
- Carbs: 30 g Protein: 31 g

165. Vietnamese Mixed Grill

Preparation time: 45 minutes
Cooking time: 30 minutes
Serving: 4
Ingredients:

- 1 1/2 lb. chicken breast
- 1 to 2 lb. flat iron or sirloin steak
- 1 1/2 lb. extra-large shrimp

Marinade ingredients:

- 2/3 cup grapeseed oil (or other high smoke point oil) - 2/3 cup rice wine vinegar
- 3 tbsp. brown sugar - 4 tbsp. fish sauce
- 4 tbsp. oyster sauce - 3 tbsp. hoisin sauce
- 1 tbsp. soy sauce - 1 tbsp. lemongrass, chopped (or 1 tbsp. lemongrass paste found in the produce section)
- 1 tbsp. Sambal Oelek or Asian chili paste
- 5 garlic cloves, chopped - 2 tsp. black pepper

Vietnamese dipping sauce ingredients:

- 1/4 cup fish sauce - 2 tsp. sugar
- 1/4 cup lime juice   1/3 cup water
- 3 garlic cloves, minced
- 1/2 tsp. chilis, finely sliced (Thai Bird, Serrano or Jalapeno)

Directions:

1. **Making the marinade:** Combine all the ingredients of the marinade in a blender and process until smoothened. Whisk the ingredients in a medium bowl and then set it aside. This marinade will make 2 cups. **Marinating the meats:** Start to pour the marinade over chicken and steak (about 1/3 cup each). Marinate in the fridge for at least 2 hours or overnight. Marinate the shrimp for just 15 to 20 minutes before grilling. **Grilling the meats on the Ninja:** Remove the meats from the fridge and marinade, letting as much drip off as possible. Preheat Ninja Foodie Grill on high. Then using grape seed, avocado, or canola oil brush, the grill grates and grill the chicken for 14 minutes flipping it halfway through. The steak will take 7 to 9 minutes. Again, flip it halfway through. Finally, grill the shrimp for 3 minutes. You can flip it if

you like. Remember to brush the grates before you add new meat.
2. **Making the Vietnamese dipping sauce (Nuoc Cham):** Blend all ingredients in a bowl good for dipping. Adjust the seasonings according to the taste. Add chili to taste.

Nutrition:

- Calories: 530 Fat: 11.3 g
- Carbs: 2 g Protein: 105 g

166. Ginger Salmon with Cucumber Lime Sauce

Preparation time: 30 minutes
Cooking time: 10 minutes **Serving:** 10
Ingredients:

- 1 tbsp. grated lime zest - 4 tsp. sugar
- 1/2 tsp. salt - 1/4 cup lime juice
- 2 tbsp. olive oil - 2 tbsp. rice vinegar or white wine vinegar - 1/2 tsp. ground coriander
- 1/2 tsp. freshly ground pepper
- 2 tsp. minced fresh ginger root
- 2 garlic cloves, minced
- 2 medium cucumbers, peeled, seeded, and chopped - 1/3 cup chopped fresh cilantro
- 1 tbsp. finely chopped onion

Salmon:

- 1 tbsp. olive oil - 1/2 tsp. salt
- 1/3 cup minced fresh ginger root
- 1 tbsp. lime juice 1/2 tsp. freshly ground pepper
- 10 salmon fillets (6 oz. each)

Directions:

1. Place the first 13 ingredients of the list in a blender. Cover and process until pureed.
2. In a bowl, combine ginger, oil, salt, lime juice, and pepper. Rub over the flesh side of salmon fillets. Lightly oil the grill. Place salmon on grill, skin side down. Grill while covered over medium-high heat for 10 to 12 minutes or until fish just begins to flake easily with a fork. Serve with sauce.

Nutrition:

- Calories: 324 Fat: 20 g Carbs: 7 g Protein: 29 g

167. Crab and Shrimp Stuffed Sole

Preparation time: 25 minutes
Cooking time: 10 to 15 minutes
Serving: 4
Ingredients:

- 2 tbsp. whipped cream cheese
- 2 tsp. minced chives
- 1 garlic clove, minced
- 1 can (6 oz.) crabmeat, drained, flaked and cartilage removed
- 1/2 cup chopped cooked, peeled shrimp
- 1/4 cup soft bread crumbs
- 1/4 cup butter, melted, divided
- 1 tsp. grated lemon zest
- 1-1/2 cups cherry tomatoes
- 2 tbsp. dry white wine or chicken broth
- 1 tsp. minced fresh parsley
- 4 sole fillets (6 oz. each)
- 2 tbsp. lemon juice
- 1/2 tsp. salt
- 1/2 tsp. pepper

Directions:

1. In a small bowl, put the crab, shrimp, bread crumbs, 2 tbsp. butter, cream cheese, chives, garlic, lemon zest, and parsley. Spoon about 1/4 cup of stuffing onto each fillet; roll up and secure with toothpicks.
2. Put each fillet on a double thickness of heavy-duty foil (about 18x12 in.). Mix up the tomatoes, wine, lemon juice, salt, pepper, and remaining butter; spoon over fillets. Fold foil around fish and seal tightly.
3. Preheat the grill for 8 minutes before grilling anything. Grill while covered over medium heat for 12 to 15 minutes or until fish flakes easily with a fork. Open the foil slowly and carefully to allow steam to escape.

Nutrition:

- Calories: 352 Fat: 16 g Carbs: 6 g
- Protein: 46 g

168. Teriyaki Salmon

Preparation time: 15 minutes
Cooking time: 8 minutes
Serving: 4
Ingredients:

- 4 salmon fillets (6 oz. each), uncooked
- 1 cup teriyaki marinade
- Oil spray, for greasing

Directions:

1. Marinate the fish fillets in the teriyaki sauce for 1 hour in the refrigerator.
2. Meanwhile, insert the grill grate in the ninja food grill and select the grill function.
3. Remember to grease the grill grate with oil spray.
4. Set the time to MAX for 10 minutes, by selecting the grill function.
5. Select start to begin preheating.
6. Once the timer beeps add fillets to the grill grate and cook for 6 minutes at MAX.
7. If the desired doneness is not achieved let it grill for 2 more minutes.
8. Then serve and enjoy hot.

Nutrition:

- Calories: 349
- Fat: 12.4 g
- Sodium: 1028 mg
- Carbs: 22.5 g
- Fiber: 0 g
- Sugar: 20 g
- Protein: 37 g

169. Grilled Citrusy Halibut

Preparation time: 15 minutes
Cooking time: 10 minutes
Serving: 4
Ingredients:

- 1 tsp. lemon zest
- 2 tbsp. lemon juice
- Salt and black pepper, to taste
- 1/2 tsp. ginger, minced
- 1 tsp. garlic, minced
- 4 tbsp. canola oil
- 2 tbsp. parsley, minced
- 2 tbsp. maple syrup
- 2 halibut fillets (6 oz. each)
- Oil spray

Directions:

1. First, insert the grill grate in the ninja food grill and select the grill function.
2. Remember to grease the grill grate with oil spray.
3. Set the time to MAX for 12 minutes, by selecting the grill function.
4. Select start to begin preheating.
5. Take a bowl and combine all the listed ingredients in it excluding fish.
6. Then spoon the marinade on top of the fish and let it sit for 20 minutes.
7. Once the ninja a Foodi grill timer beeps add the fillet to the grill grate.
8. Pour any extra sauce on top of the fish.
9. Let the fish grill for 10 minutes at MAX.
10. Once done, serve.

Nutrition:

- Calories: 314
- Fat: 17.5 g
- Sodium: 82 mg
- Carbs: 7.5 g
- Fiber: 0.2 g
- Sugar: 6.2 g
- Protein: 30.4 g

170. Salmon With Herbs

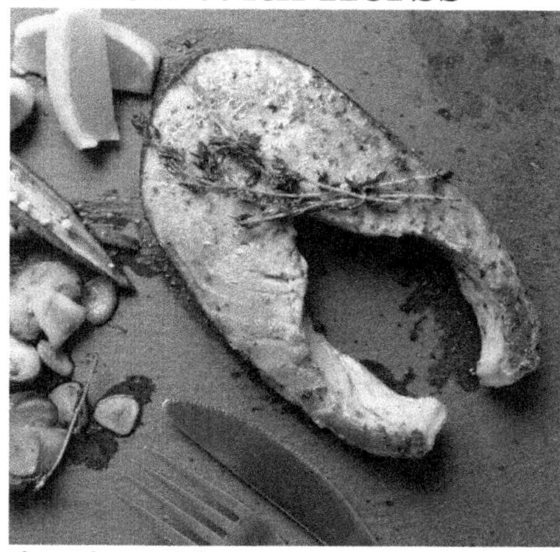

Preparation time: 15 minutes
Cooking time: 12 minutes
Serving: 2
Ingredients:

- 2 lemons, juice only
- 1/3 cup fresh mint, chopped
- 1/4 cup fresh parsley, chopped
- 1 tbsp. Dijon mustard
- 1 garlic clove
- Salt and black pepper, to taste
- 1 lb. center-cut salmon, skinned
- Oil spray

Directions:

1. Combine all the listed ingredients excluding fish in a blender and process.
2. Add a few tbsp. water if needed.
3. Once the smooth paste is formed, marinate fish in it for 30 minutes.
4. Next, insert the grill grate in the ninja food grill and select the grill function.
5. Remember to grease the grill grate with oil spray.
6. Set the time to MAX for 8 minutes, buy selecting grill function.
7. Select start to begin preheating.
8. Once done with the preheating adds fillets to the grill and close the hood.
9. GRILL at MAX, for 12 minutes.
10. Flipping is not necessary.
11. Once cooked, serve the fish.

Nutrition:

- Calories: 637
- Fat: 20
- Sodium: 433 mg
- Carbs: 2.7 g
- Fiber: 1.6 g
- Sugar: 0.2 g
- Protein: 105 g

171. Lemon Pepper Shrimp

Preparation time: 12 minutes
Cooking time: 8 minutes
Serving: 1
Ingredients:

- 10 large Shrimps
- 2 tbsp. Vegetable oil, avocado
- 1 tbsp. Lemon pepper seasoning.
- Oil spray

Directions:

1. Coat the shrimp with vegetable oil and lemon pepper seasoning
2. Rub it all well.
3. Next, insert the grill grate in the ninja food grill and select the grill function.
4. Remember to grease the grill grate with oil spray.
5. Set the time to MAX for 8 minutes, buy selecting grill function.
6. Select start to begin preheating.
7. Once the unit is preheated add the fish to the grill grate and close the hood
8. Grill at MAX for 8 minutes.
9. Flipping the shrimp is not necessary.
10. Once done, serve.

Nutrition:

- Calories: 263
- Fat: 16 g
- Sodium: 270 mg
- Carbs: 3.7 g
- Fiber: 0.9 g
- Sugar: 0 g
- Protein: 25.4 g

172. Glazed Salmon

Preparation time: 15 minutes
Cooking time: 10 minutes
Serving: 2
Ingredients:

- 1/2 tbsp. lemon pepper
- 1 /2 tbsp. everything bagel seasoning
- Pinch of salt
- 1 tsp. old bay seasoning
- 2 tbsp. butter
- 2 salmon fillets, 8 oz. each
- 1 tbsp. honey
- Oil spray

Directions:

1. Insert the grill grate in the ninja food grill and select the grill function.
2. Remember to grease the grill grate with oil spray.
3. Set the time to MAX for 8 minutes, buy selecting grill function.
4. Select start to begin preheating.
5. Take a bowl and mix honey with melted butter, old bay seasoning, salt, bagel seasoning, and lemon pepper.
6. Mix well and coat the fish with the glaze evenly.
7. Once coated, wait for the unit to get preheated
8. One beef sound, add the fillets to the grill grate and close the hood.
9. Grill at max for 8 minutes.
10. Once done, serve and enjoy.

Nutrition:

- Calories: 373
- Fat: 22.6 g
- Sodium: 239 mg
- Carbs: 9.7 g
- Fiber: 0.4 g
- Sugar: 8.6 g
- Protein: 34.9 g

173. Smoked Shrimp

Preparation time: 15 minutes
Cooking time: 7 minutes
Serving: 1
Ingredients:

- 10 large shrimps
- 1 tsp. smoked paprika
- 1 tsp. thyme, dry
- Pinch of salt
- 1/4 tsp. garlic powder
- 1/4 onion powder
- 1/2 tsp. cayenne pepper
- 1/4 tsp. lemon zest
- Oil spray

Directions:

1. Insert the grill grate in the ninja food grill and select the grill function.
2. Remember to grease the grill grate with oil spray.
3. Set the time to MAX for 8 minutes, buy selecting grill function.
4. Select start to begin preheating.
5. Mix the entire rub and spices in a bowl and then coat the shrimp with the spice rub.
6. Spray the shrimp with oil spray and transfer it to the grill grate.
7. Let it grill at MAX for 7 minutes.
8. Flipping is not necessary.
9. Once it's done, serve.

Nutrition:

- Calories: 80
- Fat: 1.4 g
- Sodium: 291 mg
- Carbs: 3.8 g
- Fiber: 1.5 g
- Sugar: 0.5 g
- Protein: 13.2 g

174. Salmon With Creamy Lime Sauce

Preparation time: 20 minutes
Cooking time: 8 minutes
Serving: 2
Ingredients:
Sauce ingredients:

- 1 tbsp. lime zest, grated - 4 tsp. brown sugar
- Salt, to taste - 1/3 cup lime juice
- 4 tbsp. olive oil - 2 tbsp. white wine vinegar
- 1/3 tsp. coriander
- 1/3 cup chopped fresh cilantro
- 1 tbsp. finely chopped onion
- 1 tbsp. chopped tomatoes - 2 cups Greek yogurt

Salmon ingredients:

- 1 tbsp. olive oil - 1/4 tsp. salt
- 1/4 cup minced fresh ginger root
- 2 tbsp. lime juice
- 1/4 tsp. freshly ground pepper
- 4 salmon fillets (6 oz. each)
- Oil spray, for greasing

Directions:

1. Take a bowl and combine all the listed sauce ingredients.
2. Mix it well and set it aside for further use.
3. Now take a separate bowl and add salt, lime juice, pepper, ginger, and olive oil.
4. Rub the fish fillet with the mixture.
5. Grease the fillets with oil spray.
6. Insert the grill grate in the ninja food grill and select the grill function.
7. Remember to grease the grill grate with oil spray.
8. Set the time to MAX for 8 minutes, buy selecting grill function. Select start to begin preheating.
9. Once done with preheating add fillets in batches into the grill and let it cook at MAX for 8 minutes, per batch.
10. Once done, serve hot with sauce.

Nutrition:

- Calories: 1330 Fat: 62 g Sodium: 473 mg
- Carbs: 28.6 g Fiber: 0.3 g Sugar: 27.5 g
- Protein: 164.5 g

175. Salmon With Cream Cheese

Preparation time: 15 minutes
Cooking time: 8 minutes
Serving: 2
Ingredients:

- 4 salmon fillets, 6 oz. each
- 6 oz. cream cheese
- 2 tbsp. mayonnaise
- 2 tsp. parsley, chopped
- 2 tsp. lemon juice
- Salt and black pepper to taste
- Oil spray, for greasing

Directions:

1. Cut the salmon fillet into small pieces and season it with salt, black pepper, and grease it with oil spray.
2. Insert the grill grate in the ninja food grill and select the grill function.
3. Remember to grease the grill grate with oil spray.
4. Set the time to MAX for 8 minutes, buy selecting grill function.
5. Select start to begin preheating.
6. Once beeps sound add salmon to the grill and grill it at MAX for 8 minutes.
7. Meanwhile, take a bowl and combine parsley, lemon zest, salt, mayonnaise, cream cheese in a bowl.
8. Serve the cooked fillet with creamy sauce and enjoy.

Nutrition:

- Calories: 829
- Fat: 56.9 g
- Sodium: 515 mg
- Carbs: 6 g
- Fiber: 0.1 g
- Sugar: 1.2 g
- Protein: 75.5 g

176. Sea Food Omelet

Preparation time: 12 minutes
Cooking time: 6 minutes
Serving: 1
Ingredients:

- 10 large shrimp, shells removed and chopped
- 4 eggs, beaten
- 1/3 cup of black olives, chopped
- Pinch of paprika
- Salt and black pepper, to taste
- Oil spray, for greasing
- 2 tbsp. coconut milk

Directions:

1. Crack eggs in a bowl and pour in the coconut milk.
2. Whisk both the ingredients well
3. Now add black olives, salt, paprika, and pepper to the eggs.
4. Mix well and add shrimp.
5. Take a small cake pan and grease it with oil spray.
6. Pour the egg mixture inside it and top it with diced shrimp.
7. Add the cake pan to the crisper basket and insert it into the unit.
8. Press AIR CRISP function and let it cook for 6 minutes, at 375°F.
9. Once done, sprinkle cheese on top and let it air crisp for 2 more minutes.
10. Serve it hot.

Nutrition:

- Calories: 640
- Fat: 33.8 g
- Sodium: 1179 mg
- Carbs: 9.4 g
- Fiber: 2.2 g
- Sugar: 2.4 g
- Protein: 73.4 g

177. Shrimp Poppers

Preparation time: 12 minutes
Cooking time: 7 minutes
Serving: 2
Ingredients:

- 1 lb. shrimp (455 g), deveined and peeled

Seasoned flour:

- 1 cup flour (125 g)
- 1 tbsp. Cajun seasoning
- 2 tsp. salt
- 1 tsp. black pepper

Egg mixture ingredients:

- 1 egg
- 3 tbsp. milk
- 1 tsp. Cajun seasoning

Directions:

1. Take a small bowl and whisk the egg in it then add Cajun seasoning and milk to the egg mixture.
2. Whisk it well and set it aside for further use.
3. In a separate bowl mix together Cajun seasoning, salt, pepper, and flour.
4. Set it aside as well.
5. Now dip the shrimp first in egg wash then in flour mixture.
6. Once all the shrimps are coated let it sit in the refrigerator for 20 minutes.
7. Add the crisper basket and insert it into the unit.
8. Press the AIR CRISP function and let it preheat for 10 minutes at 375°F.
9. Then grease the crisper plate with oil spray.
10. Add the coated shrimp to the basket and let it air crisp at 375°F for 7 minutes.
11. Once all the shrimps are done, serve.

Nutrition:

- Calories: 543
- Fat: 7.1 g
- Sodium: 2997 mg
- Carbs: 53.1 g
- Fiber: 2 g
- Sugar: 1.4 g
- Protein: 62 g

178. Pineapple Fish Fillet

Preparation time: 15 minutes
Cooking time: 7 minutes
Serving: 2
Ingredients:

- 1 tsp. Chili powder as needed
- 1/ 2 cup cilantro leaves, chopped
- 1 tbsp. lime juice
- Salt and black pepper to taste
- 1/2 tbsp. canola oil
- 2 fillet salmon, 6-8 oz.
- 2 tbsp. pineapple juice, fresh squeezed
- 1 cup grilled pineapple slices

Directions:

1. Take a blender and pulse cilantro with canola oil.
2. Add salt and black pepper.
3. Then add the lime juice, chili powder, and pineapple juice.
4. Now rub the fillet with the blended mixture.
5. Pre-heat your Ninja Foodi Grill to MAX set a timer to 12 minutes.
6. Once preheating is done, grill the fillets and grill for 7 minutes.
7. Once done serve it with grilled pineapple.

Nutrition:

- Calories: 320
- Fat: 14.3 g
- Sodium: 115 mg
- Carbs: 4.8 g
- Fiber: 0.9 g
- Sugar: 3.7 g
- Protein: 44.5 g

179. Coconut Battered Fish Fillets

Preparation time: 15 minutes
Cooking time: 10 minutes
Serving: 2
Ingredients:

- Salt and pepper to taste
- 1/2 tsp. mustard powder
- 2 tsp. garlic powder
- 1/3 cup plain flour
- 1 cup coconut flour
- Oil spray, for greasing
- 2 fish fillets, salmon (6 oz. each)

Directions:

1. Insert the grill grate in the ninja food grill and select the grill function.
2. Remember to grease the grill grate with oil spray.
3. Set the time to MAX for 8 minutes, buy selecting grill function.
4. Select start to begin preheating.
5. Meanwhile, mix salt, pepper, mustard powder, garlic powder, plain flour, and coconut flour in a bowl.
6. Season the fish with salt and black pepper and coat it with oil spray.
7. Once the unit is preheated add the fish to the grill grate and grill at MAX for 10 minutes
8. No need to flip the fillets.
9. Once it's done serve.

Nutrition:

- Calories: 333
- Fat: 12.9 g
- Sodium: 500 mg
- Carbs: 37.7 g
- Fiber: 3.9 g
- Sugar: 1.3 g
- Protein: 17.2 g

180. Spiced up Grilled Shrimp

Preparation time: 5 to 10 minutes
Cooking time: 6 minutes
Serving: 4
Ingredients:

- 2 tbsp. brown sugar
- 1 lb. jumbo shrimp, peeled and deveined
- 2 tbsp. olive oil
- 1 tbsp. garlic powder
- 1 tbsp. paprika
- 1/2 tsp. black pepper
- 1 tsp. garlic salt

Directions:

1. Take a bowl and add listed ingredients gently mix
2. Let the mixture chill for 30 to 60 minutes
3. Preheat your Grill in MED mode setting the timer to 6 minutes
4. Once you hear the beep, arrange your prepared shrimp over the grill grate
5. Lock and let it cook for 3 minutes
6. Flip and cook for 3 minutes more
7. Once done, serve and enjoy!

Nutrition:

- Calories: 370
- Fat: 27 g
- Sat fat: 3 g
- Carbs: 23 g
- Fiber: 8 g
- Sodium: 182 mg
- Protein: 6 g

181. Mustard-y Crisped up Cod

Preparation time: 5 to 10 minutes
Cooking time: 10 minutes
Serving: 3
Ingredients:

- 1 large whole egg
- 1 tsp. Dijon mustard
- 1/2 cup bread crumbs
- 1 lb. cod filets
- 1/4 cup all-purpose flour
- 1 tbsp. dried parsley
- 1 tsp. paprika
- 1/2 tsp. pepper

Directions:

1. Take fish fillets and slice them into 1-inch-wide strips
2. Take a mixing bowl and whisk in eggs, add mustard and combine well
3. Add flour to another bowl
4. Take another bowl and add bread crumbs, dried parsley, paprika, black pepper and combine well
5. Coat strips with flour, then coat with egg mix, coat with crumbs at last
6. Preheat Ninja Foodi by pressing the "AIR CRISP" option and setting it to "390°F" and timer to 10 minutes
7. Let it preheat until you hear a beep
8. Arrange strips directly inside basket, lock lid, and cook until the timer runs out
9. Serve and enjoy!

Nutrition:

- Calories: 200
- Fat: 4 g
- Sat fat: 1 g
- Carbs: 17 g
- Fiber: 1 g
- Sodium: 214 mg
- Protein: 24 g

CHAPTER 9:

Desserts

182. Creamy Mango Cake

Preparation time: 5 to 10 minutes
Cooking time: 30 minutes
Serving: 8 to 10
Ingredients:

- 2 cups white flour
- 1/2 cup sugar
- 2 mangoes, peeled and cubed
- 6 eggs, whisked
- 1 cup heavy cream
- 1 tsp. vanilla extract
- 1 tsp. baking powder
- Cooking spray

Directions:

1. Take a cake pan, grease it with some cooking spray, vegetable oil, or butter. Add the ingredients and combine well.
2. Take Ninja Foodi multi-cooker, arrange it over a cooking platform, and open the top lid. In the pot, add water and place a reversible rack inside the pot. Place the pan over the rack. Close the multi-cooker by locking it with the Crisping Lid, ensure to keep the pressure release valve locked/sealed.
3. Select "BAKE/ROAST" mode and adjust the 350°F temperature level. After that set timer to 30 minutes, then press "STOP/START," it will start the cooking process by building up inside pressure. Once the timer goes off, quickly release pressure by adjusting the pressure valve to the VENT.
4. When the pressure gets released, open the Crisping Lid. Slice the cake and serve warm.

Nutrition:

- Calories: 301
- Fat: 14 g Sat fat: 7 g
- Trans fat: 0 g Carbs: 26.5 g
- Fiber: 2 g
- Sodium: 153 mg
- Protein: 6 g

183. Easy Pineapple Cake

Preparation time: 5 to 10 minutes
Cooking time: 40 minutes
Serving: 8 to 10
Ingredients:

- 2 oz. chocolate chips
- 12 oz. canned pineapple, crushed
- 14 oz. cake mix

Directions:

1. Take a cake pan, grease it with some cooking spray, vegetable oil, or butter. Add the ingredients and combine well.
2. Take Ninja Foodi multi-cooker, arrange it over a cooking platform, and open the top lid.
3. In the pot, add water and place a reversible rack inside the pot. Place the pan over the rack.
4. Close the multi-cooker by locking it with the Crisping Lid, ensure to keep the pressure release valve locked/sealed.
5. Select "BAKE/ROAST" mode and adjust the 350°F temperature level. After that, set the timer to 40 minutes then press "STOP/START," it will start the cooking process by building up inside pressure.
6. Once the timer goes off, quickly release pressure by adjusting the pressure valve to the VENT.
7. When the pressure gets released, open the Crisping Lid. Slice the cake and serve warm.

Nutrition:

- Calories: 258
- Fat: 8 g
- Sat fat: 1 g
- Trans fat: 0 g
- Carbs: 36 g
- Fiber: 3 g
- Sodium: 125 mg
- Protein: 3 g

184. Chocolate Pudding

Preparation time: 5 to 10 minutes
Cooking time: 20 minutes
Serving: 4
Ingredients:

- 2 eggs, whisked
- 2 tsp. butter, melted
- 1 cup dark chocolate, melted
- 16 oz. cream cheese
- 2 tbsp. sugar
- Cooking spray

Directions:

1. Take 4 ramekins, grease them with some cooking spray, vegetable oil, or butter. In a bowl, whisk all the ingredients and add in the ramekins.
2. Take Ninja Foodi multi-cooker, arrange it over a cooking platform, and open the top lid.
3. In the pot, add water and place a reversible rack inside the pot. Place the pan over the rack.
4. Close the multi-cooker by locking it with the Crisping Lid, ensure to keep the pressure release valve locked/sealed.
5. Select "BAKE/ROAST" mode and adjust the 340°F temperature level. After that, set the timer to 20 minutes then press "STOP/START," it will start the cooking process by building up inside pressure.
6. Once the timer goes off, quickly release pressure by adjusting the pressure valve to the VENT.
7. When the pressure gets released, open the Crisping Lid. Slice the cake and serve warm.

Nutrition:

- Calories: 523 Fat: 28 g
- Sat fat: 11 g
- Trans fat: 0 g
- Carbs: 44 g
- Fiber: 2 g
- Sodium: 421 mg
- Protein: 12 g

185. Chocolate Peanut Butter and Jelly Puffs

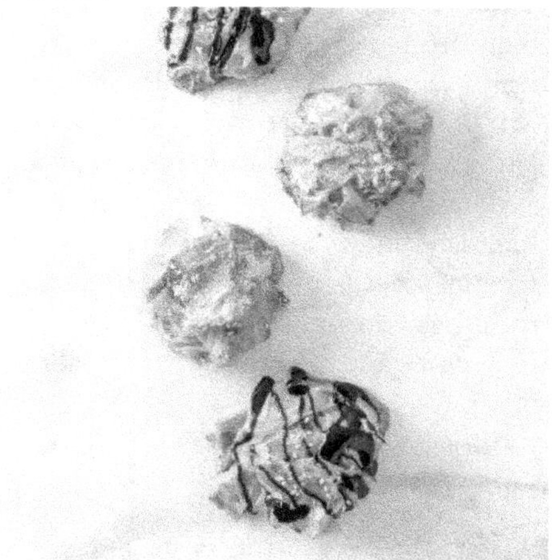

Preparation time: 25 minutes
Cooking time: 15 minutes
Serving: 4
Ingredients:

- 1 (16 oz.) tube prepared flaky biscuit dough
- 2 (1 1/2 oz.) milk chocolate bars
- Cooking spray
- 16 tsp. (about 1/3 cup) creamy peanut butter
- 1 cup confectioners' sugar - 1 tbsp. whole milk
- 1/4 cup raspberry jam

Directions:

1. Remove biscuits from the tube. There is a natural width-wise separation in each biscuit. Gently peel each biscuit in half using this separation.
2. Break the chocolate into 16 small pieces.
3. Spray a baking sheet with cooking spray.
4. Using your hands, stretch a biscuit half until it is about 3-inches in diameter. Place a tsp. of peanut butter in the center of each biscuit half, then place a piece of chocolate on top.
5. Pull an edge of dough over the top of the chocolate and pinch together to seal. Continue pulling the dough over the top of the chocolate and pinching it until the chocolate is completely covered. The dough is pliable, so gently form it into a ball with your hands.
6. Place on the prepared baking sheet. Repeat this step with the remaining biscuit dough, peanut butter, and chocolate.
7. Place the baking sheet in the refrigerator for 5 minutes.
8. Place Cook and Crisp Basket in the pot. Close crisping lid. Choose Air Crisp, fix temperature to 360°F, and time to 20 minutes. Select Start/Stop to begin. Let preheat for 5 minutes.
9. Remove the biscuits from the refrigerator and spray the tops with cooking spray. Open the lid and spray the basket with cooking spray.

10. Place 5 biscuit balls in the basket. Close lid and cook for 5 minutes.
11. When cooking is complete, remove the biscuit balls from the basket. Repeat step 7 two more times with the remaining biscuit balls.
12. Mix together the confectioners' sugar, milk, and jam in a small bowl to make a frosting.
13. When the cooked biscuit balls are cool enough to handle, dunk the top of each into the frosting. As frosting is beginning to set, garnish with any toppings desired, such as sprinkles, crushed toffee or candy, or mini marshmallows.

Nutrition:
- Calories: 663
- Fat: 25 g
- Sat fat: 8 g
- Cholesterol: 5 mg
- Sodium: 1094 mg
- Carbs: 101 g
- Fiber: 3 g
- Protein: 14 g

186. Red Velvet Cheesecake

Preparation time: 10 minutes
Cooking time: 25 minutes
Serving: 8
Ingredients:
- 2 cups Oreo cookie crumbs
- 3 tbsp. unsalted butter, melted
- 2 packages cream cheese, at room temperature
- 1/2 cup granulated sugar
- 1/2 cup buttermilk
- 2 tbsp. unsweetened cocoa powder
- 1 tsp. vanilla extract
- 2 tbsp. red food coloring
- 1/2 tsp. white vinegar
- 1 cup water

Directions:
1. In a small bowl, blend the cookie crumbs and butter. Press this mixture into the bottom of the Ninja Multi-Purpose Pan or 8-inch baking pan. In a huge bowl, use an electric hand mixer to blend the cream cheese, sugar, buttermilk, cocoa powder, vanilla, food coloring, and vinegar for 3 minutes. Pour this over the cookie crust. Cover the pan tightly with aluminum foil.
2. Place the water in the pot. Insert Reversible Rack into the pot, making sure it is in the lower position. Place the covered multi-purpose pan onto the rack. Attach pressure lid, ensuring the pressure release valve is in the SEAL position.
3. Select PRESSURE on HI. Set time to 25 minutes. Press Start/Stop to begin. Once done cooking, let the pressure naturally release for 15 minutes. After 15 minutes, quickly release any pressure remaining by turning the pressure release valve to the VENT position. Cautiously remove the lid when the unit has finished releasing pressure. Remove cheesecake from the pot. Leave in the refrigerator for 3 hours, or overnight if possible before serving.

Nutrition:
- Calories: 437
- Fat: 31 g
- Sat fat: 18 g
- Cholesterol: 74 mg
- Sodium: 338 mg
- Carbs: 36 g
- Fiber: 3 g
- Protein: 7 g

187. Black Beans Brownies

Preparation time: 10 minutes
Cooking time: 20 minutes
Serving: 12
Ingredients:

- 4 oz. Chocolate, chopped.
- 4 eggs; whisked.
- 1 cup white flour
- 1/2 cup canned black beans; drained, and blended
- 1/2 cup butter, melted
- 1/4 cup brewed black coffee
- 1 1/4 cups sugar
- 1 tsp. vanilla extract
- Cooking spray

Directions:

1. In a bowl, put and combine all the ingredients except the cooking spray and whisk well.
2. Grease a cake pan with the cooking spray and pour the batter into it
3. Put the reversible rack in the Foodi, add the cake pan inside, set the machine on baking mode, and cook at 350°F for 20 minutes. Slice the brownies and serve.

Nutrition:

- Calories: 233
- Protein: 5.52 g
- Fat: 11.64 g
- Carbs: 26.58 g

188. Cocoa and Orange Pudding

Preparation time: 10 minutes
Cooking time: 20 minutes
Serving: 4
Ingredients:

- 1 egg
- 2 tbsp. orange juice
- 4 tbsp. white flour
- 1 tbsp. cocoa powder
- 4 tbsp. sugar
- 2 tbsp. coconut oil, melted
- 4 tbsp. milk
- 1/2 tsp. baking powder
- 1/2 tsp. lime zest; grated.

Directions:

1. In a bowl, mix all the ingredients, stir well and divide into 4 ramekins.
2. Put the reversible rack in the Foodi, put the ramekins inside, set the machine on baking mode, and cook 320 for 20 minutes. Serve the pudding warm.

Nutrition:

- Calories: 188
- Protein: 5.42 g
- Fat: 11.48 g
- Carbs: 16.93 g

189. Apple Pie

Preparation time: 5 minutes
Cooking time: 55 minutes
Serving: 8
Ingredients:

- 2 apples, cored, peeled, and sliced
- 2 eggs; whisked.
- 3/4 cup milk
- 2/3 cup white flour
- 1/3 cup sugar
- Cooking spray
- 2 tbsp. flavored liqueur
- 1 tsp. cinnamon powder

Directions:

1. In a bowl, mix the sugar with the cinnamon, flour, eggs, milk, and the liqueur and stir well.
2. Grease the Foodi's cake pan with cooking spray and arrange the apples into the pan
3. Pour the batter over the apples and put the pan in the Foodi.
4. Set the machine on baking mode and cook at 400°F for 55 minutes. Cool the pie down, slice, and serve.

Nutrition:

- Calories: 136
- Protein: 5.07 g
- Fat: 4.1 g
- Carbs: 20.16 g

190. Apple Jam

Preparation time: 10 minutes
Cooking time: 20 minutes
Serving: 6
Ingredients:

- 1 lb. apples, peeled, cored, and chopped
- 2 lb. sugar
- 2 cups apple juice
- Juice of 2 limes

Directions:

1. In your Foodi, combine all the ingredients, toss, put the pressure lid on and cook on High for 20 minutes.
2. Blend the mixture using an immersion blender, divide into cups and serve cold.

Nutrition:

- Calories: 683
- Protein: 1.41 g
- Fat: 1.26 g
- Carbs: 171.87 g

191. Pineapple and Yogurt Cake

Preparation time: 10 minutes
Cooking time: 40 minutes
Serving: 6
Ingredients:

- 5 oz. flour
- 1 egg; whisked.
- 1/2 cup sugar
- 1/3 cup coconut flakes, shredded
- 1/4 cup pineapple juice
- 4 tbsp. vegetable oil
- 3 tbsp. yogurt
- 3/4 tsp. baking powder
- 1/2 tsp. baking soda
- 1/2 tsp. cinnamon powder
- Cooking spray

Directions:

1. In a bowl, put and mix all the ingredients except the cooking spray and whisk well. Grease the Foodi's cake pan with cooking spray and pour the cake batter inside
2. Put the reversible rack in the Foodi, put the cake pan on the rack, set the machine on baking mode, and cook the cake at 320°F for 40 minutes. Cool down, cut, and serve it.

Nutrition:

- Calories: 267
- Protein: 5.47 g
- Fat: 13.49 g
- Carbs: 31.4 g

192. Chocolate Cookies

Preparation time: 15 minutes
Cooking time: 15 minutes
Serving: 4
Ingredients:

- 250 g (8.81 oz.) flour
- 2 eggs
- 100 g (3.52 oz.) butter
- 5 tbsp. sugar
- 8 g (0.28 oz.) baking powder
- 80 g (2.82 oz.) dark chocolate drops
- Honey to taste
- Sugar grains to taste

Directions:

1. In a bowl, mix the butter, flour, sugar, and eggs and begin to knead.
2. Add the chocolate chips and finally the baking powder.
3. Work the mix until smooth and homogeneous.
4. Preheat the Ninja Foodi to 180°F.
5. Take some of the mixtures and start making balls by placing them inside the basket of the Ninja Foodi.
6. When the unit is ready, select "Air Fry'" and bake for 15 minutes.
7. When ready, brush with honey and add the granulated sugar.
8. Repeat from step 5 until the dough is done.
9. Let them cool and serve.

Nutrition:

- Calories: 497
- Fat: 25.2 g
- Carbs: 66.1 g
- Protein: 4.6 g.

193. Sweet Cream Cheese Wontons

Preparation time: 5 minutes
Cooking time: 5 minutes
Serving: 16
Ingredients:

- 1 egg mixed with a bit of water
- Wonton wrappers to taste
- 1/2 cup powdered erythritol
- 8 oz. softened cream cheese
- Olive oil to taste

Directions:

1. Mix sweetener and cream cheese.
2. Layout 4 wontons at a time and cover with a dish towel to prevent drying out.
3. Place 1/2 of 1 tsp. cream cheese mixture into each wrapper.
4. Dip a finger into the egg/water mixture and fold diagonally to form a triangle. Seal edges well.
5. Repeat with the remaining ingredients.
6. Select AIR FRYER, set the temperature to 400°F, and set the time to 5 minutes. Select START/STOP to start preheating.
7. Air fry. Place filled wontons into the air fryer and cook 5 minutes at 400°F, shaking halfway through cooking.

Nutrition:

- Calories: 303
- Fat: 3 g
- Protein: 1 g
- Sugar: 4 g

194. Smoked Apple Crumble

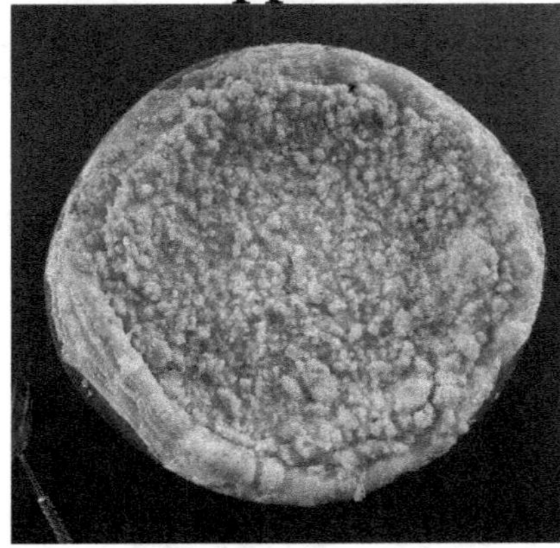

Preparation time: 5 minutes
Cooking time: 45 minutes
Serving: 4
Ingredients:

- 4 to 5 large Honeycrisp apples, peeled and sliced
- Juice from 1/2 lemon
- 2 tbsp. flour
- 1/3 cup sugar
- 1 tbsp. ground cinnamon
- 1 tsp. ground nutmeg

For the topping:

- 1 cup brown sugar
- 1/2 cup All-purpose flour
- 1/2 cup oats
- 1/4 cup walnuts
- Salt to taste
- 1 1/2 tsp. cinnamon
- 8 tbsp. butter

Directions:

1. Select BAKE, set the temperature to HIGH, and set the time to 45 minutes. Select START/STOP to start preheating.
2. Place the apples in a large mixing bowl and toss with lemon juice. Then add in flour, sugar, cinnamon, and nutmeg. Mix thoroughly.
3. Pour the apples into a pot. Set the mixture aside.
4. Using the now-empty mixing bowl, combine brown sugar, flour, oats, walnuts, cinnamon, and salt for the topping.
5. Using a pastry blender or large fork, cut the cold butter into the topping mix.
6. Cover the apples with a topping mixture.
7. Place the apple crumble inside the unit.
8. Close the hood and bake it for about 45 minutes. Serve it warm with vanilla ice cream.

Nutrition:

- Calories: 317 Fat: 11 g
- Protein: 3 g
- Sugar: 5 g

195. Bread Pudding With Cranberry

Preparation time: 5 minutes
Cooking time: 35 minutes
Serving: 4
Ingredients:

- 2 1/2 eggs
- 1/2 cup cranberries
- 1 tsp. butter
- 1/4 cup and 2 tbsp. white sugar
- 1/4 cup golden raisins
- 1/8 tsp. ground cinnamon
- 3/4 cup heavy whipping cream
- 3/4 tsp. lemon zest
- 3/4 tsp. kosher salt
- 3/4 French baguettes, cut into 2-inch slices
- 3/8 vanilla bean, split and seeds scraped away
- Cooking spray

Directions:

1. Lightly grease the baking pan of the air fryer with cooking spray. Spread baguette slices, cranberries, and raisins.
2. In a blender, blend well vanilla bean, cinnamon, salt, lemon zest, eggs, butter, sugar, and cream. Pour over the baguette slices. Let it soak for an hour.
3. Cover the pan with foil.
4. For 35 minutes, cook at 330°F.
5. Let it rest for 10 minutes. Serve it and enjoy.

Nutrition:

- Calories: 590
- Fat: 25 g
- Protein: 17 g
- Sugar: 9 g

196. Baked Apple

Preparation time: 5 minutes
Cooking time: 20 minutes
Serving: 4
Ingredients:

- 1/4 cup water
- 1/4 tsp. nutmeg
- 1/4 tsp. cinnamon
- 1 1/2 tsp. melted ghee
- 2 tbsp. raisins
- 2 tbsp. chopped walnuts
- 1 medium apple

Directions:

1. Select AIR FRYER, set the temperature to 350°F and the time to 20 minutes. Select START/STOP to start preheating.
2. Slice the apple in half and discard some of the flesh from the center.
3. Place into the frying pan.
4. Mix the remaining ingredients, except for water. Spoon the mixture to the middle of apple halves.
5. Pour water over the filled apples.
6. Air fry. Place the pan with the apple halves into the air fryer, bake for 20 minutes.

Nutrition:

- Calories: 205
- Fat: 11 g
- Protein: 2 g
- Sugar: 5 g

197. Coffee and Blueberry Cake

Preparation time: 5 minutes
Cooking time: 35 minutes
Serving: 6
Ingredients:

- 1 cup white sugar
- 1 egg
- 1/2 cup butter softened
- 1/2 cup fresh or frozen blueberries
- 1/2 cup sour cream
- 1/2 tsp. baking powder
- 1/2 tsp. ground cinnamon
- 1/2 tsp. vanilla extract
- 1/4 cup brown sugar
- 1/4 cup chopped pecans
- 1/8 tsp. salt
- 1 1/2 tsp. confectioners' sugar for dusting
- 3/4 cup and 1 tbsp. all-purpose flour
- Cooking spray

Directions:

1. In a small bowl, whisk well the pecans, cinnamon, and brown sugar.
2. In a blender, blend well all the wet ingredients. Add the dry ingredients, except for the confectioner's sugar and blueberries. Blend well until smooth and creamy.
3. Lightly grease the baking pan with cooking spray.
4. Pour half of the batter into the pan. Sprinkle half of the pecan mixture on top. Pour the remaining batter. And then top with the remaining pecan mixture.
5. Cover the pan with foil.
6. Bake for 35 minutes; cook at 330°F.
7. Serve and enjoy with a dusting of confectioner's sugar.

Nutrition:

- Calories: 480
- Fat: 26 g
- Protein: 5 g
- Sugar: 8 g

198. Fried Bananas

Preparation time: 5 minutes
Cooking time: 10 minutes
Serving: 2 to 3
Ingredients:

- 1 cup panko breadcrumbs
- 1/2 cup almond flour
- 3 egg whites
- 8 ripe bananas
- 3 tbsp. vegan coconut oil

Directions:

1. Heat coconut oil and add breadcrumbs. Mix around 2 to 3 minutes until golden. Pour into a bowl.
2. Peel and cut the bananas in half. Roll half of each banana into flour, eggs, and crumb mixture.
3. Air fry. Place it into the air fryer. Cook for 10 minutes at 280°F.
4. A great addition to a healthy banana split!

Nutrition:

- Calories: 215
- Fat: 11 g
- Protein: 5 g
- Sugar: 5 g

199. Lemon Berry Cake

Preparation time: 5 minutes
Cooking time: 3 hours 15 minutes
Serving: 4
Ingredients:

- 6 eggs
- 1/2 cup coconut flour
- 1/3 cup lemon juice
- 2 tsp. zest
- 1 tsp. lemon liquid stevia
- 1/2 cup Swerve sweetener
- 2 cups heavy cream
- 1/2 tsp. salt
- 1/2 cup fresh blueberries

Directions:

1. Place the egg whites into a stand mixer and whip until stiff peaks form. Set it aside.
2. In another bowl, whisk the yolks and the remaining ingredients together, except blueberries.
3. Fold the egg whites a little at a time into the batter until just combined.
4. Grease your Ninja Foodi pot and pour the mixture. Sprinkle the blueberries over the batter.
5. Cover the lid and Bake on LOW for 3 hours or until a toothpick comes out clean.
6. Allow cooling with the cover off for 1 hour, then place it in the refrigerator to chill for 2 hours.
7. Serve it cold with whipped cream if desired.

Nutrition:

- Calories: 191
- Fat: 17 g
- Fiber: 4 g
- Carbs: 4 g
- Protein: 4 g

200. Cherry Cake

Preparation time: 5 minutes
Cooking time: 3 hours 40 minutes
Serving: 12
Ingredients:

- 1 box of chocolate cake mix
- 21 oz. canned cake pie filling
- 1 1/2 cups cola
- 8 oz. cream cheese icing from a 16 oz. store-bought container

Directions:

1. Turn your Ninja Foodi on and place cherry pie filling, spreading evenly.
2. Spread the cake mix as a layer, spread evenly, and be as smooth as possible on the cherry pie filling.
3. Slowly add the cola over the dry cake mix, 1/2 cup at a time. Make sure all the dry cake mix is covered with cola.
4. Cover the lid and cook on HIGH for 3 1/2 to 4 hours.
5. Turn off the Ninja and allow it to sit uncovered for 1/2 hour.
6. Serve the cake on plates and drizzle it with cream cheese icing.
7. Serve it with whipped cream or vanilla ice cream as desired.

Nutrition:

- Calories: 415
- Fat: 15 g
- Fiber: 3 g
- Carbs: 69 g
- Protein: 4 g

201. Peach Dump Cake

Preparation time: 5 minutes
Cooking time: 2 hours 15 minutes
Serving: 6
Ingredients:

- 14.5 oz. canned peach
- Box yellow cake mix
- 1 cup butter melted

Directions:

1. Turn on your Ninja Foodi and grease the bottom.
2. Add canned peach with the juice.
3. Sprinkle the dry cake mixes with the butter on the top of the peach as evenly as possible.
4. Cover the lid, set to bake.
5. Cook on HIGH for 2 hours.
6. Frost with favorite frosting.
7. Enjoy!

Nutrition:

- Calories: 619
- Fat: 35 g
- Fiber: 0 g
- Carbs: 74 g
- Protein: 3 g.

202. Easy Blueberry Cobbler

Preparation time: 10 minutes
Cooking time: 1 hour 5 minutes
Serving: 8
Ingredients:

- 1 cup self-rising flour
- 1 cup milk
- 1/2 cup butter
- 1 cup white sugar
- 4 cup fresh blueberries

Directions:

1. Select "Bake" and preheat your Ninja Foodi to 350°F.
2. Put butter to use in an 8-inch square baking dish
3. Then, melt the butter in the preheating unit for like 5 minutes and then remove it from the unit.
4. Mix sugar, flour, and milk in a bowl until combined. Then pour the batter over the melted butter and scatter the blueberries over the batter.
5. Bake in the already preheated unit until you insert a toothpick at the center and it comes out clean in approximately 1 hour.

Nutrition:

- Calories: 310.4
- Carbs: 48.5 g
- Protein: 3.2 g
- Fat: 12.5 g
- Cholesterol: 32.9 mg
- Sodium: 293.4 mg.

203. Grilled Pineapple Butterscotch Sundaes

Preparation time: 10 minutes
Cooking time: 25 minutes
Serving: 12
Ingredients:

- 2 tbsp. white sugar
- 2 fresh pineapples to be peeled, cored, and cut into 6 spears
- 1 cup packed brown sugar
- 6 tbsp. butter
- 1/4 tsp. ground nutmeg
- 1/2 cup butter
- 1/2 cup heavy whipping cream
- Pinch of salt
- 1 tsp. vanilla extract
- 3 cup vanilla ice cream

Directions:

1. Preheat the grill with medium heat and lightly oil the grate
2. Heat 6 tbsp. butter, nutmeg, and white sugar in a saucepan on medium heat and stir until the sugar dissolves in about 5 minutes. Then brush the pineapple spears with butter mixture.
3. Arrange the pineapple on the already preheated grill and cover, grill until it becomes lightly brown, turning frequently; this should last between 7 to 10 minutes. Then transfer the pineapple to a platter.
4. Get another saucepan and melt the remaining 1/2 cup of butter using medium heat. Stir in the heavy cream and brown sugar, then bring to a boil, stirring as frequently as possible. Remove from the heat and add salt and vanilla extract. Serve the pineapple topped with ice cream and cream sauce.

Nutrition:

- Calories: 388.2 Carbs: 51.9 g
- Protein: 2.7 g Fat: 21 g
- Cholesterol: 63.7 mg Sodium: 131.2 mg

204. Classic Dinner Rolls

Preparation time: 40 minutes
Cooking time: 20 minutes
Serving: 12
Ingredients:

- 1 envelope yeast
- 1/2 tsp. salt
- 1/4 cup water
- 2 cups all-purpose flour or more if necessary
- 2 tbsp. sugar
- 1/2 cup milk
- 2 tbsp. butter or margarine

Directions:

1. Combine 3/4 cup of flour, sugar, undissolved yeast, and salt in a large bowl. Heat butter, water, and milk until they become very warm (120°F to 130°F). Then add to the flour mixture. Beat for 2 minutes with a medium speed of electric mixer, scraping the bowl frequently. Add 1/4 cup of flour and beat for 2 minutes at high speed. Stir in the remaining flour to make a soft dough. Knead on a lightly floured surface until it becomes smooth and elastic in about 8 to 10 minutes. Cover and let it rest for about 10 minutes.
2. Divide the dough into 12 equal pieces and shape them into balls. Then put in a greased 8-inch round pan. Cover and let it rise in a warm daft-free place until it becomes doubled in about 30 minutes.
3. Cook in the already preheated 375°F Ninja Foodi, "Bake" mode, for 20 minutes or until it gets done. Remove from the pan and brush with extra melted butter if you like. Serve it warm.

Nutrition:

- Calories: 107.9
- Carbs: 18.5 g
- Protein: 2.8 g
- Fat: 2.3 g
- Cholesterol: 5.9 mg
- Sodium: 115.3 mg

205. Chantal's New York Cheesecake

Preparation time: 30 minutes
Cooking time: 1 hour
Serving: 12
Ingredients:

- 2 tbsp. butter to be melted
- 1 1/2 cup white sugar
- 4 large eggs
- 15 large rectangular pieces or either 2 squares or 4 small rectangular pieces of graham crackers to be crushed
- 4 (8 oz.) packages of cream cheese
- 3/4 cup milk
- 1 cup sour cream
- 1/4 cup all-purpose flour
- 1 tbsp. vanilla extract

Directions:

1. Preheat the Ninja Foodi to 350°F. Then grease a 9-inch springform pan.
2. Get a medium bowl and mix the melted butter with graham cracker crumbs. Then, press on the bottom of the springform pan.
3. Get a large bowl and mix sugar with cream cheese until they become smooth. Blend in milk, and after that, mix the eggs one after the other and let it incorporate. Then mix in vanilla, sour cream, and flour until they become smooth. Then pour filling into the prepared crust.
4. Bake in the already preheated Ninja for like 1 hour. Turn off the Ninja and leave the cake to cool in it while the unit door is closed for about 5 to 6 hours; this is necessary to prevent cracking. Then chill in the refrigerator until you are ready to serve.

Nutrition:

- Calories: 533.4 Carbs: 44.2 g
- Protein: 10.3 g Fat: 35.7 g
- Cholesterol: 158.9 mg Sodium: 380.4 mg

206. Cinnamon Sugar Muffins

Preparation time: 15 minutes
Cooking time: 20 minutes
Serving: 6
Ingredients:

- 1/2 cup erythritol sweetener
- 5 tbsp. butter, softened
- 1 tsp. vanilla
- 2 eggs
- 1/2 cup half and half
- 1 1/2 cups almond flour
- 1 tbsp. ground flaxseed
- 2 tsp. baking powder
- 1 tsp. cinnamon
- 1/2 tsp. ginger
- 1/2 tsp. nutmeg

Cinnamon sugar:

- 4 tbsp. butter, melted
- 1/2 cup granulated erythritol
- 2 tsp. cinnamon

Directions:

1. Preheat the Ninja Foodi Grill on the "Bake" mode at 350°F.
2. Mix all the muffin ingredients in a bowl until smooth.
3. Divide this muffin batter in a greased muffin tray.
4. When the grill is preheated, open its hood and place the muffin tray in it.
5. Cover the grill's hood and bake these muffins for 20 minutes.
6. Mix cinnamon with butter and sweetener in a bowl and drizzle over the muffins.
7. Serve.

Nutrition:

- Calories: 118 Fat: 20 g
- Sodium: 192 mg Carbs: 6.8 g
- Fiber: 0.9 g
- Sugar: 19 g
- Protein: 5.2 g

207. Blueberry Muffins

Preparation time: 15 minutes
Cooking time: 20 minutes
Serving: 6
Ingredients:

- 2 1/2 cup blanched almond flour
- 1/2 cup erythritol
- 1 1/2 tsp. baking powder
- 1/4 tsp. sea salt
- 1/3 cup coconut oil
- 1/3 cup unsweetened almond milk
- 3 large eggs
- 1/2 tsp. vanilla extract
- 3/4 cup blueberries

Directions:

1. Preheat the Ninja Foodi Grill on the "Bake" mode at 350°F.
2. Mix all the muffin ingredients except berries, in a bowl until smooth.
3. Fold in blueberries and divide this muffin batter in a greased muffin tray.
4. When the grill is preheated, open its hood and place the muffin tray in it.
5. Cover the grill's hood and bake these muffins for 20 minutes.
6. Serve.

Nutrition:

- Calories: 248
- Fat: 16 g
- Sodium: 95 mg
- Carbs: 8.4 g
- Fiber: 0.3 g
- Sugar: 10 g
- Protein: 14.1 g

CHAPTER 10:

4-Week Diet Plans

1st week:

DAY	BREAKFAST	LUNCH	SNACKS	DINNER
1	Bacon on The Grill	Garlicky Lemongrass Chicken	Wrapped Stuffed Jalapenos	Grilled Cauliflower with Miso Mayo
2	Grilled Ham	Grilled Chicken Breasts with Lemon	Grilled Guacamole	Grilled Cauliflower Wedges with Herb Tarator
3	Grilled Fried Eggs	Big Bob Gibson's Chicken	Zucchini Cheese Roulades	Grilled Green Tomatoes
4	Cheesy Eggs	Baja-Style Rosemary Chicken Skewers	Grilled Zucchini with Chicken	Grilled Carrots with Avocado and Mint
5	Grilled Sausages	Piri Piri Chicken	Bacon Jalapenos	Grilled Eggplant with Tahini-Yogurt Sauce
6	Grilled Breakfast Sausage	Grilled Chicken Thighs	Grilled Eggplant Parmesan	Mushrooms with Béarnaise Yogurt
7	Avocado Eggs	Grilled Chicken with Chimichurri	Wrapped Shrimp	Grilled Green Beans

2nd week:

DAY	BREAKFAST	LUNCH	SNACKS	DINNER
1	Bacon on The Grill	Lacquered Rib Eye	Wrapped Stuffed Jalapenos	Taco Lime Shrimp
2	Grilled Ham	Skirt Steak with Ba Sauce	Grilled Guacamole	Cilantro Lime Grilled Salmon
3	Grilled Fried Eggs	Tri-Tip Steak with Tiger Bite Sauce	Zucchini Cheese Roulades	Grilled Lobster Tail
4	Cheesy Eggs	Soy Sauce–Marinated Grilled Flank Steak	Grilled Zucchini with Chicken	Grilled Tilapia with Tomatoes
5	Grilled Sausages	Grilled Brisket with Scallion-Peanut Salsa	Bacon Jalapenos	Lemony Grilled Salmon
6	Grilled Breakfast Sausage	Grilled Rib Eye with Shishito Pepper Salsa	Grilled Eggplant Parmesan	Grilled Halibut with Avocado Salsa
7	Avocado Eggs	Grilled Bone-In Rib Eye	Wrapped Shrimp	Spicy Grilled Fish

3rd week:

DAY	BREAKFAST	LUNCH	SNACKS	DINNER
1	Grilled Egg with Prosciutto and Parmesan	Grilled Chicken with Mustard Sauce	Mushroom Bacon Bites	Jalapeño Poppers with Smoked Gouda
2	Grilled Ham	Grilled Red Curry Chicken	Grilled Guacamole	Grilled Asparagus
3	Grilled Fried Eggs	Grilled Chicken and Radishes	Zucchini Cheese Roulades	Grilled Broccoli
4	Cheesy Eggs	Grilled Chicken with Olives	Grilled Zucchini with Chicken	Grilled Fish Steaks
5	Grilled Sausages	Tamarind-Glazed Chicken Wings	Bacon Jalapenos	Double Chocolate Muffins
6	Grilled Breakfast Sausage	Coconut and Lemongrass Steak Skewers	Grilled Eggplant Parmesan	Hot Shot Salmon
7	Avocado Eggs	Hasselback Short Rib Bulgogi	Wrapped Shrimp	Chili-Lime Grilled Salmon

4th week:

DAY	BREAKFAST	LUNCH	SNACKS	DINNER
1	Grilled Egg with Prosciutto and Parmesan	Flank Steak with Zucchini Salsa	Mushroom Bacon Bites	Spicy Grilled Fish
2	Grilled Ham	Coconut-Marinated Short Rib Kebabs	Grilled Guacamole	Spicy Grilled Shrimp
3	Grilled Fried Eggs	Grilled Beef with Broccoli	Zucchini Cheese Roulades	Grilled Chicken Thighs
4	Cheesy Eggs	Hawaiian Rib-Eye Steak	Grilled Zucchini with Chicken	Grilled Chicken with Chimichurri
5	Grilled Sausages	Jalapeño-Marinated Pork Chops	Bacon Jalapenos	Grilled Chicken with Olives
6	Grilled Breakfast Sausage	Pork Chops with Radishes	Grilled Eggplant Parmesan	Mushrooms with Béarnaise Yogurt
7	Avocado Eggs	Grilled Pork Ribs with Gochujang Sauce	Wrapped Shrimp	Grilled Eggplant with Tahini-Yogurt Sauce

CHAPTER 11:

2–4 Week Diet Plans

1st week:

DAY	BREAKFAST	LUNCH	SNACKS	DINNER
1	Butternut Squash with Italian Herbs	Bourbon Pork Chops	Baked Apple	Italian Stuffed Pork Chops
2	Stuffed up Bacon and Pepper	Breaded Pork Chop	Coffee and Blueberry Cake	Kewpie-Marinated Chicken
3	Epic Breakfast Burrito	Broccoli Crisp	Cinnamon Fried Bananas	Leg of Lamb
4	Energetic Bagel Platter	Buttered Leg of Lamb	Lemon Berry Cake	Lemon Pepper Shrimp
5	Morning Frittata	Cheese Stuffed Zucchini	Cherry Cake	Lemony Green Beans
6	Breakfast Potato Casserole	Chicken Breasts with Pineapple Relish	Peach Dump Cake	Marinated Grill Chicken Breast
7	Avocado Eggs	Chicken Cheese Patties	Easy Blueberry Cobbler	Mashed Asparagus

2nd week:

DAY	BREAKFAST	LUNCH	SNACKS	DINNER
1	Sausage with Eggs	Delicious Maple-Glazed Chicken	Baked Apple	Meatball Sandwiches with Mozzarella and
2	Veggie Packed Egg Muffin	Easy BBQ Roast Shrimp	Coffee and Blueberry Cake	Mexican Street Corn
3	Bacon-Herb Grit	Eggplant with Greek yogurt	Grilled Pineapple Butterscotch Sundaes	Mustard Green Veggies
4	Cinnamon Oatmeal	Filet Mignon with Pineapple Salsa	Classic Dinner Rolls	Mustard-y Crisped up Cod
5	Spinach Tater Tot Casserole	Garlic and Sage Tomatoes	Chantal's New York Cheesecake	Nutty Acorn Squash
6	Ninja Foodi Bean	Gazpacho Salsa	Cinnamon Sugar Muffins	Paprika Grilled Shrimp
7	Kale and Sausage Delight	Generous Pesto Beef Meal	Blueberry Muffins	Parmesan, Cheddar, And Zucchini Casserole

3rd week:

DAY	BREAKFAST	LUNCH	SNACKS	DINNER
1	Ninja Foodi Breakfast Sausages	Perfect Spanish Garlic Shrimp	Apple Pie	Simple Beef Tenderloin
2	Ninja Foodi Swiss-Cheese Sandwiches	Peruvian Chicken Skewers	Apple Jam	Simple Lamb Chop
3	Ninja Foodi Bacon Bombs	Pineapple Fish Fillet	Pineapple and Yogurt Cake	Smoked Shrimp
4	Ninja Foodi Bread and Bacon Cups	Piri Piri Chicken	Chocolate Cookies	Soy and Garlic Steak Kebabs
5	Ninja Foodi Breakfast Frittata	Ranch Pork Chops	Sweet Cream Cheese Wontons	Spiced Up Grilled Shrimp
6	Ninja Foodi Cinnamon Buttered Toasts	Roast Beef with Garlic	Smoked Apple Crumble	Spice-Rubbed Duck Breast
7	The Broccoli and Maple Mix	Roasted Cauliflower	Bread Pudding with Cranberry	Spinach Chickpea Stew

4th week:

DAY	BREAKFAST	LUNCH	SNACKS	DINNER
1	Banana Oat Muffins	Stuffed Tomatoes	Creamy Mango Cake	Marinated Grill Chicken Breast
2	Delicious Berry Oatmeal	Sweet and Sour Chicken BBQ	Easy Pineapple Cake	Mashed Asparagus
3	Greek Egg Muffins	Sweet Potato Fingers	Chocolate Pudding	Meatball Sandwiches with Mozzarella and
4	Breakfast Skewers	Teriyaki Salmon	Chocolate Peanut Butter and Jelly Puffs	Mexican Street Corn
5	Campfire Hash	Teriyaki-Marinated Salmon	Red Velvet Cheesecake	Mustard Green Veggies
6	Grilled Honeydew	The Tarragon Chicken Meal	Black Beans Brownies	Mustard-y Crisped Up Cod
7	Zesty Grilled Ham	Tofu with Orange Sauce	Cocoa and Orange Pudding	Nutty Acorn Squash

Conclusion

This post was created to teach you about the Ninja Foodi grill and how it may complement your cooking passion. First, we will cover the different features of this grilling gear and why they might be valuable for you. After this, we will take a look at some ideas on how to use the equipment for different types of food such as meats, vegetables, and fish. Finally, we will wrap up by giving you some helpful tips on buying off the internet or in-store, as well as maintenance tips that won't break your budget.

Ninja Foodi is a company that offers cooking gear designed specifically with home enthusiasts in mind. The main products from the company are the grills which we will go over next.

The grills range in size and shape but ultimately, they all do the same thing: allow you to cook delicious food without worrying about any mess or hassle. By having a grill that is easy to use and clean you can enjoy your time cooking no matter how much experience you have.

Each of these options has its own set of features, such as temperature control, steaks, and so on, but the way they've been created is the main distinction. For example, their temperature control is much higher when cooking at a high temperature than it is when cooking at a low temperature. This allows the user to change the temperature levels quickly without having to wait for the entire trip through all of its settings.

This comes in handy when you want to change your food's atmosphere during your cooking process to accommodate different temperatures or if you want to make sure that food will stay warm while you grill something else over it (i.e., veggies).

The Ninja Foodi Grill brings a health-conscious and budget-friendly experience to food preparation. The grill uses an electric heating element that can cook, bake, and roast everything from vegetables to pizza. The device comes with a steamer insert for healthy cooking that is worth the investment—and it's actually fun! The grill will cost less than three hundred dollars and comes in two designs: stainless steel or black matte.

Ninja Foodi Grills are innovative devices for cooking healthy meals without destroying your wallet or your waistline. It's as simple as turning on this grill to cook a meal, even if you're inexperienced with cooking like me.

The Ninja Foodi Grill is designed for health-conscious consumers who value quality over quantity. It cooks foods in a safe and healthy way in minutes, which allows you to make grilling fun. The Ninja Grill also saves you money by eliminating the need to buy expensive ingredients. The steamer insert takes all of the guesswork out of healthy cooking, leaving you with nutritious food that tastes great!

The Ninja Grill is not only a healthier option for your wallet—it's also fun! I was first hesitant to purchase this device since I thought the concept was absurd…

I was mistaken. Ninja Foodi Grills are a great investment, especially if you consider the health of your family.